Sweet Caroline

Sweet Caroline

Miriam Hamilton

MERCIER PRESS

IRISH PUBLISHER – IRISH STORY

MERCIER PRESS

Cork

www.mercierpress.ie

© Miriam Hamilton, 2012

ISBN: 978 1 85635 935 1

10 9 8 7 6 5 4 3 2 1

A CIP record for this title is available from the British Library

Printed and bound in the EU.

Contents

This book is dedicated to Colin, who has supported and encouraged me throughout all we have been through; to David, Paul and Samuel, my adorable boys; and of course to Caroline, my beautiful and brave daughter.

1

THE GOOD NEWS

There is definitely a sixth sense in women. It is not really a feeling; it's even more innate than that. It is a gut instinct that tells you to do a pregnancy test *now*, right away. I got that sense on a rainy, depressing Monday in January 2008 as I left school at lunchtime to get a coffee and a break from the back-to-school chaos that accompanies a new term. No matter how long they have been in schools, most teachers of teenagers would agree that on the first day back after holidays they feel a hint of trepidation, which they overcome by marching into the first class of the day and getting on with the drama of their teaching life. The morning had gone okay for me, except for the niggling feeling that I had to get to a pharmacy to do a pregnancy test. It was ridiculous, really; my husband Colin and I had decided quite quickly over Christmas that we would love to have one more baby and, since I had just turned thirty-seven, it seemed unlikely that we would be lucky enough not to have to wait at least a few months. As I walked towards the shops, I found myself wondering whether there was any point in wasting money on a test, as my period was not due for a few days. But I knew myself well enough to realise this attempt at being rational was futile; I walked on into the pharmacy, led firmly by my gut, and promptly bought a pregnancy test.

I then went to a small café and ordered a coffee, finding myself asking for a decaf to be healthy (just in case), and went off to the ladies to do the test. Back at my table, I sipped at my coffee for the few minutes the test would take, and then, as covertly as was possible in a full café, sneaked a glance at the result. For a few seconds I had the sinking feeling I've always had when a pregnancy test has been negative – the pink line I was looking for in the test's second viewing window didn't appear. With a pregnancy test, however, it seems impossible to take just one look at the result and put it away. I found myself examining it more carefully, turning and twisting the testing stick around in the light, almost wishing for the line – which would indicate a positive test – to appear. Then I thought I saw something, as the light caught the testing stick from one angle in particular. I raced outside to check more carefully. Sure enough, the faintest line imaginable *was* visible in the second window. I could not believe it and stood for a moment in total surprise. An excited smile began to spread across my face as I thought,

'Welcome, baby number four.' Little did I know at that moment that this little baby was going to turn our lives upside down.

***

Colin and I had started our family in 2000 with the birth of our son David. This first pregnancy introduced me to the wonderful world of internal examinations, being dry shaved in the nether regions by a complete stranger, and the joys of the pre-op enema. David was delivered by elective Caesarean section a week early, as he was in a breech position – intending to be born feet first instead of head first. Everyone advised me that it would be best if I chose to be awake for the delivery. My advisers were mostly male doctors, anaesthetists and women who had no children or who had experienced only natural deliveries. Even my own husband insisted it would feel more like a real birth experience if I was awake. That I agreed to this reveals, I suppose, my clearly significant levels of 'baby brain' – a temporary period of naivety some pregnant women experience, which included, in my case, unerring trust in the instincts of everyone but myself.

Yes, I had a real – and memorable – birth experience all right, but a terrifying one. I had experienced nothing quite like that long-awaited delivery day: willingly walking into an operating theatre, with all manner of glistening silver instruments on view, and propping myself up on a narrow table to have a spinal block inserted into my back before I willingly lay down, wide awake, while I was cut open and had my baby hauled out. I'm sorry: I cannot romanticise the experience in any way, because for me it was horrifying.

It was not that there was any sensation of pain, but the manoeuvring to get the baby out was certainly uncomfortable and frightening, and I had read far too many books, so I was completely tuned in to every step. Throughout the whole operation – from realising for the first time, as they put the blue screen right up in front of my face to block the view, that I have claustrophobia issues, to hearing the sounds of the suctioning and knowing that they were removing the amniotic fluid around the baby – I shook with fear. The staff were brilliant, especially the anaesthetist, who tried to keep me calm. But I told myself that if I had another child I would love to give birth naturally, despite the pain, and that if I ever had to have a Caesarean section again I would insist on being under a general anaesthetic, sound asleep.

David was handed to me to breastfeed, but by this time I was so heavily sedated I could barely keep my eyes open to see him, let alone feed him. He was very handsome, however, like his dad, and I did bond with him soon afterwards, once the drugs and adrenaline coursing through my veins had dissipated. He was a healthy 7 lb 5 oz (3.32 kg), delivered at thirty-nine weeks on 31 October. He is our little warlock, with his Hallowe'en birthday.

Our second son, Paul, arrived in 2002, just nineteen months after David, and, as planned, I insisted on a natural delivery. I did have to push this slightly (pardon the pun) at the hospital, as there were worries that I had a slightly increased risk of uterine rupture, having previously had a Caesarean birth. I had done lots of research on vaginal birth after Caesarean and found that the risks were marginal, as long as the delivery was monitored carefully throughout. Having signed all the forms indicating I was aware of the risks, I prepared myself for my first vaginal delivery. I had an internal examination (often simply called 'an internal') on the day Paul was due, and was informed that my cervix was already two centimetres dilated – my cervix was beginning to open and labour was impending. I was pleased with this news as the long pregnancy was coming to an end and I was looking forward to my baby's arrival. I went home with the advice that it would only be a matter of days before labour would begin.

That evening I experienced a bit of bloody mucus, commonly called a 'show', but this was to be expected after the internal, so I went to bed unconcerned at ten o'clock, with a Harry Potter book. Colin had already been demoted to the spare room, as I was by now extremely large and needed the whole bed in which to manoeuvre and spread out comfortably at night. At about eleven o'clock I heard a popping sound. My first thought was that Colin was having a bottle of champagne on his own (an early celebration of the birth of our baby) without me, in the spare room. Then it dawned on me that we had no champagne in the house – we rarely do – and, besides, Colin was snoring audibly next door. My second thought was that I was having a terrible accident, as I felt warm liquid flowing down below. My third was the realisation that my waters must have broken: I had no control of the liquid, which by now was soaking the bed. I jumped up, as athletically as I could at forty weeks' gestation, and grabbed the sleeping bag I had luckily put on the bed earlier that evening. I then hobbled, with the bag gathering fluid at a fast rate and getting heavier with every step, out to the hall to try to wake Colin. He wouldn't wake. Reluctant to wake David, who was obliviously sleeping further down the hall, I had to squeeze very inelegantly through the bedroom door and give Colin a kick. After a few minutes he was up and we were on our way to the hospital.

I felt every bump on the journey, as by now I was experiencing light pains and the baby's head was banging down on my cervix without the fluid to cushion it. We got to the hospital at midnight, and I was advised to get into my bed and sleep. I was far too excited for that. I walked up and down the aisle of the ward to get things going. This proved to be quite entertaining, as there were other women who had also clearly read the pregnancy books about the powers of gravity and movement in progressing labour, doing the same thing. We would exchange apprehensive but knowing glances as we silently passed each other on the corridor, lean against the wall when the contraction hit, and then shuffle along again. I remember wondering whether there might be a need for a 'Hospital Ward Walking Policy' if pregnancies continued rising in number as they had in recent years – a sort of rules-of-the-road-type thing: 'Women must give way to other women coming out of the ward, or overtake on the right, never inside, to allow for a contracting woman who is hogging the hard shoulder.' Within about six hours I had dilated to a significant enough degree to be shipped to the labour ward for some pain relief.

Going through the labour ward to get to my delivery room was like being in the scene in the film *The Silence of the Lambs* in which Clarice Starling passes along the cells on death row and the awful noises and sounds frighten her. It was noisy, and for the first time I heard the primal screams of women nearing the end of their labours and pushing their babies out. The midwife saw my face and advised me to try not to take any notice of the screaming, saying, 'Everyone deals with the pain differently.'

We passed room after room on the way to the delivery bay where I would spend the coming hours. The staff there gave me the gas and air – sometimes referred to as laughing gas – commonly used as mild pain relief during labour. The gas and air was great fun for a while, until it – or the pain of the contractions, I am not sure which – made me feel really sick. By eight o'clock I was insisting I needed an epidural (spinal block) because I didn't think I could cope with much more. I think I expected labour pains to be like a dull ache, as I had heard so many times that they were like period pains but a lot worse. For me they started out like that, but soon I was surprised by their sharpness: they felt like the combination of a bad ache with the pain of a sharp knife cutting right down onto my cervix. I remember thinking that the gallstone pain I had had a few years earlier was the only pain even vaguely resembling this. Yet this pain felt productive: I could feel it pushing my cervix painfully apart and therefore I could rationalise it to some degree. I remembered reading all the books that warned mothers not to panic as the pain intensified. Yet that was exactly what I did. Negative feelings that I couldn't possibly live through this began infiltrating my thoughts. I desperately awaited an epidural.

By ten o'clock the next morning, the anaesthetist had administered the epidural, and I felt great. Initially it left me with only slight tightening as I contracted, but no pain. I was so relaxed I could flick through a magazine and chat, because the contractions were no worse than the practice Braxton Hicks contractions – mild, usually painless, contractions or tightening of the uterus, which occur in many women near the end of a pregnancy – I had already experienced. I was really happy and looking forward to a pain-free end to the birth.

A few hours into the epidural, however, I began to feel pains that worsened steadily. I mentioned them to the midwives, who checked my back and realised that in turning over during labour I must have detached the tube inserted there to administer the epidural drugs. It would be a few hours before the anaesthetist – occupied by an emergency Caesarean section in an operating theatre – could replace it. All hell broke loose for me then, in terms of pain. I went from the blissful situation of virtually no pain into the transition phase of labour – the final phase of dilation up to ten centimetres, prior to pushing the baby out. This is the toughest and most difficult stage for many women as the contractions are at their strongest and most frequent. It is the peak of the first stage of labour and *transitions* the mother into the next stage, when the baby is born. This was excruciating. I panicked even more than I had earlier. I was crying and fussing – not doing very well at all. I remember feeling as though my back would break. No amount of rubbing or moving around did any good. I remembered seeing the videos of women who moved around right through their labour, and I marvelled at how anyone had the strength to stand up, literally, to pain like that which I was experiencing.

By one o'clock the anaesthetist was free to attend to me, topping up the epidural as I began the pushing phase of labour – during which the pregnant woman puts her chin on her chest and pushes down into her bottom, as if passing a stool. This pushes the baby through the cervix with each contraction and into the birth canal, until eventually the baby emerges from the vagina after many long pushes. Before long Paul was crowning – beginning to emerge from the vagina with each push, but going back in between pushes. Because he was being monitored continually due to the risk of uterine rupture, the midwives discovered he was getting tired. I overheard them mentioning that they would have to intervene. I mistakenly jumped to the unwelcome conclusion they were talking about a Caesarean section, but they quickly clarified it was far too late for that. I realised they were talking about an episiotomy – a cut into the vagina to help release the baby. I begged for a few more minutes to push, arguing that an episiotomy was not part of my birth plan, in an attempt to put them off the idea. Paul was a big baby, however; Colin ventured a look down below and suggested that I might as well have the cut as I was tearing myself anyway. It wasn't the most helpful comment I have ever received in labour, but I conceded defeat. The last thing I remember seeing after the stirrups were wheeled in, and my feet were secured in them, was a doctor approaching me with a pair of scissors in one hand and a large set of silver forceps in the other. I looked away as I gave a final push and, with assistance, Paul was born. The hospital staff stitched me up while I fed my new 9-lb (4.08-kg) baby. Although vaginal childbirth had been a scary experience, I felt that through it I had completed one of the female rites of passage. I was very sore, but I was elated that Paul, my second beautiful son, had arrived.

In 2006 our third son, Samuel, was born. This time my pregnancy continued beyond the due date, so I was admitted to hospital for ARM (artificial rupture of the membranes), during which a crochet hook-like instrument is inserted into the vagina and up through the cervix to nick the amniotic membrane and release the waters so that labour can proceed. Two things made me suitable for this procedure: my cervix was again two centimetres dilated – which allowed the instrument into the vagina to nick the membrane – and I had laboured well after my waters had broken in my previous pregnancy. At three o'clock in the afternoon my waters broke, and by a quarter past seven that evening Samuel had been born. His birth was quick, intense and a very positive experience, because I harboured none of the fear or panic I had previously experienced about how bad the pain would get. This time I knew what would happen and I was prepared: I was adamant that I did not want an epidural, because I wanted to have full sensation for the pushing stage and I wanted to be back on my feet after the birth. I managed on gas and air and with the use of a TENS machine, which works on the principle of suppressing pain signals to the brain and encouraging the release of endorphins, with the effect that the sensation of the pain is diluted to some degree. I have no idea if the machine had any effect, as the labour was tough, but I was calm and went into a kind of meditative state: every time I had a contraction, I focused on a clock's small hand ticking round and just breathed slowly and deeply. I felt well in control right to the last push, when Samuel was born.

He climbed up to my breast to feed himself, which was amazing to see, and was an easy-going, relaxed baby from day one. Perhaps a calm, uneventful arrival suited him – who knows? He was fair and placid, and a happy, handsome third son. I was proud of how I had managed through his birth and thrilled with my complete family (Colin and I had decided three would be more than enough children for us to bring up). I think that is partly why I was particularly excited about my fourth pregnancy, as it was quite a spontaneous decision that was realised very quickly, which made it seem as though it was meant to be and was part of our family's fate. Of course, I had no idea of what we were to face as a family in the months that followed.

***

Once I had absorbed the positive result of the pregnancy test, I phoned Colin to tell him the news, which surprised him as much as it had me. We settled into a period of lovely evenings during which, once the children were in bed, we chatted about what life would be like having four young children. We debated whether we would have a boy or girl. Both of us felt the baby would probably be another boy, since we had had three already, and that was great. We genuinely did not mind either way, as long as the baby was healthy. We knew we would have to change our car to a seven-seater to fit in four children with their safety seats. I spent time discussing when I should take maternity leave and relished the prospect of a considerable spell of time at home with the whole family.

I had met Colin when I was studying in London and had remained there working as a teacher after qualification. When we married we decided to move to Ireland to raise a family. However, after we moved back Colin found that his career never really took off. Outside Dublin there were few opportunities for the museum and exhibition-design jobs or model-making that Colin had enjoyed for many years during a successful career in Britain. Owing to the security of my job, we were not overly concerned when work prospects were poor in Colin's area of expertise. We had always felt strongly that one of us should be a full-time carer for our children; it naturally evolved that Colin looked after the children, with a view to returning to work if an opportunity arose in our location. We had a good quality of life, as I had ample holidays to spend with the family at home and felt that work did not interfere hugely with my home life.

Before long our discussions began to focus on my age: I was thirty-seven. Colin was forty-seven, so neither of us were at an optimum age for reproduction. I was very much aware that most mothers-to-be in the over-thirty-five bracket get on well, with no problems. But I had read the literature, and all the books had a section on older mothers and how being older posed risks for both mother and baby, but particularly raised the baby's risk of problems. I was therefore also aware that I was at higher risk of conceiving a baby with an abnormality than younger women were. I had no worries around my own health, as I was fit and had been training hard as an athlete up until the time I had conceived Caroline. I was carrying no excess weight, had normal blood pressure and experienced no medical issues. I did worry, however, about the risk of my eggs' DNA being older, and therefore possibly less healthy, than that of younger women. It is easy to play down the risks of an older mother when most have no issues, but often we do not hear of the more negative stories and I was concerned. I felt lucky to have had three very healthy boys; a little bit of me felt I was tempting fate by having a fourth at this age. I decided I would discuss the issue at the hospital when I got my appointment and take it from there.

2

ANTENATAL CARE AND THE FIRST SPECIAL SCAN

My antenatal care, as is the norm, began with a visit to the family's general medical practitioner, who did the initial checks, such as weight and blood pressure, and noted dates. A letter from the maternity hospital followed, giving a date for my first scan, due when I had progressed to fourteen weeks' gestation. I was aware that the issue of miscarriage was significant up until that date. I hoped I would be all right and that the pregnancy would progress. Having had no bleeding in my previous pregnancies, I felt confident that all would be well in this area. As had been the case with the boys, I was able to enjoy the knowledge of the new pregnancy for only about two weeks until the familiar sensation of morning sickness appeared, when I was around eight weeks pregnant. This was for me the very worst symptom of the whole of pregnancy; I would wake in the morning and only five seconds would pass before the horrendous feeling of nausea would travel through my system. I would feel shaky, weak, tired and sick. The feeling would subside temporarily if I ate something there and then, but would soon be back, sometimes within half an hour. My sickness would last on and off all day. I remember having to leave the classroom where I was teaching to run to the toilets to throw up. I would return shakily to continue the lessons as if nothing had happened. I looked green for the first three months; people who knew me could tell I was pregnant.

When I got home from work I would get into pyjamas, flop on the couch and move only to go to the toilet. I had no interest in anything but passing the time until I felt well again, which I knew would take many weeks. I rarely managed to stay up past the nine o'clock evening news and, despite often having twelve hours' sleep, I would awaken exhausted. It always amazes me how babies manage to develop properly when mothers are so sick in pregnancy. It seems an evolutionary blip that a mother is not able to eat well in the crucial first trimester of her baby's development. At the same time, the nausea does force expectant mothers to take it easy, which perhaps balances things out. So, the first trimester of my fourth pregnancy, as had been the case with my earlier pregnancies, passed in a haze of nausea, exhaustion, work and sleep. My thoughts focused solely on my first scan, which would not only give me a glimpse of my baby but also herald the end of the dreaded sickness and the beginning of the enjoyable second trimester, during which things would get much better – or so I expected.

I awoke to bright sunshine on the day of my scan, still feeling wobbly but not as bad as I had been. The name of the consultant assigned to me for my pregnancy appeared on the hospital letter. I took little notice of who it was, as I had chosen, as was the case with all my pregnancies, to use public rather than private medical services. It never really entered my head to do otherwise. Going private would have meant I saw the same consultant for all my antenatal appointments in his or her private rooms, rather than at the hospital. It may have meant that the consultant would deliver me, if he or she were available, and it may have meant a private room for me. I am not a great fan of the public–private divide in our health system and believe patients should be seen according to their health needs and nothing else. Choice is fine if you have one. Private rooms should be for the sickest patients to rest in, and not for those who can buy them even if their procedure is routine. I had no problem with being in a ward with other women; in fact I believed I would enjoy chatting to them and giving and getting advice on motherhood and breastfeeding. After all, it would only be for a few days if all went well. For the previous three pregnancies I had briefly met the consultants: once or twice with David to discuss the breech-birth scenario and the need for a Caesarean section, once with Paul to sign the forms and discuss the vaginal birth after the section, and not at all with Samuel. The midwives and doctors had looked after us well and I did not expect to meet the consultant this time either.

The first hospital appointment in a pregnancy is always long, and this one was no different. I went in to speak to a midwife, who discussed my medical history, including all three previous pregnancies, in detail. Colin and I mentioned family members on both sides and any health issues of which we were aware. I have always enjoyed this bit of the appointment, as it is a bit like an informal, relaxed chat and an acknowledgement before the scan happens that I am really going to have a baby. The midwife asked me to consent to an HIV test to check for potential AIDS, and this brought home to me that I was solely responsible for maintaining a healthy lifestyle so that my baby had the best chance of a great start in life. I was soon to realise that, despite a mother's best efforts, things can go wrong.

I received my card for recording all antenatal care throughout the pregnancy. I have always sighed when getting this card at the start of a pregnancy; it is so empty at the first visit, and the time when it will be full of appointments and my baby will be due seems so far away. The room for routine checks of urine, weight and blood pressure was heaving with pregnant women. The queues at every section were long, which was frustrating as I was desperate to get to the scan room and see my baby. I had the required urine and weight checks, and copious vials of blood were taken from me for testing. I finally made it to the scanning room, where I had to begin drinking lots of water to ensure a full bladder for this important first scan. I waited about an hour and a half, and was beginning to think I would have to go to the toilet and then begin drinking all over again, when a tall, handsome man – the consultant – came in and had a word with the two inundated sonographers. He picked up a few files, presumably to give a hand in clearing the backlog of waiting women. I looked at Colin and said, 'Maybe we will get to meet the consultant, which would give me a great opportunity to ask a few questions regarding my age.' Just then, the tall man called my name. Colin and I went in for our scan.

The consultant welcomed us and proceeded to do the scan. He was very attentive and appeared to have a good look at the baby, telling us that everything seemed fine at this stage. He asked how I was feeling. When I mentioned I was still feeling sick he said that this was a good sign, because it indicated pregnancy hormones were high. I asked lots of questions and raised the issue of my age, which he did not dismiss and chatted about the option of an amniocentesis to rule out any major chromosomal abnormalities. This procedure involves extracting a small amount of amniotic fluid from around the baby in the womb. The fluid is then sent for examination of the chromosomes that are shed from the baby into the fluid. This examination checks for major chromosomal abnormalities, such as Down's syndrome or Edwards' syndrome. The consultant explained that at my age the risk of miscarriage due to the procedure almost exactly equalled the chance of there being an abnormality: 1 in 200. He talked to us about which would be worse for us – having a child with an abnormality or losing a healthy baby through miscarriage due to the procedure. I asked him if there were any signs of abnormality on the scan and, although he said there were not, he emphasised that this was a very early scan and that not much could be gleaned from it. He advised us to think carefully through the decision on an amniocentesis and to let him know what we would like to do.

Just before we left, the consultant asked me about my dates and whether I ever had long menstrual cycles. I said I did occasionally have a longer cycle but would usually get my period within a few days of my expected date, never longer than that. I asked why he was checking. He mentioned in an unconcerned tone that the baby was measuring twelve weeks and five days instead of fourteen weeks, as per my dates. For the first time in the pregnancy I felt an uneasy sensation spread through my body. I didn't emerge from the consultation euphoric, as I had done in previous pregnancies. Something felt different. I can clearly remember a sense of foreboding. I knew my dates were spot on, and I knew instinctively from that moment that all was not well. Colin tried to reassure me that nothing was amiss, but I knew he was wrong. It was the strongest gut reaction I have ever felt, and from that moment on not a single day went by on which I did not worry about our baby's health.

The pregnancy continued uneventfully for a number of weeks. The biggest change for me was the cessation of the pregnancy sickness. Colin and I talked about the tests and whether we should go for them or take a chance. I was not keen on the amniocentesis as I was nervous of miscarriage, and at the time we were adamant that even if we found out something was wrong we didn't think we would be able to go through a termination.

At the back of my mind all the time were the dates and why the baby was a week or so behind in development. I had been fairly healthy from the start of the pregnancy, but three things concerned me. First, I was worried because I had conceived over the Christmas holidays and had drunk some alcohol on my birthday and Christmas Day before I had known I was pregnant. I was apprehensive that I might have done harm. Second, I was concerned because I had gone for a run the day after probable conception and, since I had been feeling good, I had pushed myself. I had come home and had had that head-exploding overheating most sportspeople will be familiar with when they have worked very hard. I worried that the temperature rise might have affected mitosis of the cells or hormones or enzymes. Third, I was worried about the effect of a nasty vomiting bug that I had had at nine or ten weeks into the pregnancy, which had involved very high temperatures. These three things played on my mind as possibly having had an effect on the baby's development, or indeed the development of the placenta in the early stages.

3

OUR BABY
IS NOT GROWING

We decided definitely not to go for the amniocentesis because of the miscarriage risk and to have an anomaly scan instead at around nineteen weeks. This way there would be no risk to the baby, but if something was spotted we could decide then what to do. An anomaly scan is essentially another scan, done later than the first fourteen-week scan, that enables a better examination of the baby because of the baby's increased size and greater development. Rather than just dating the gestational age of the baby, an anomaly scan enables further measurements, for example of the nuchal fold in the neck, which may indicate some conditions, such as Down's syndrome. The baby's heart and other organs can also be looked at, so this type of scan gives a good indicator of the health of the baby in so far as this is possible from outside the womb.

During the scan everything appeared to be fine with the baby, until the measurements were collated at the end. It was then that the consultant mentioned that the baby was measuring around fifteen weeks' gestation, with a very abnormal weight-for-age of only 4 oz (125 g). The weight should have been closer to 10 oz at this stage. The baby was now only just over the size it should have been at my first scan (approximately 110 g), yet I was approaching the midpoint of my pregnancy. Of course, I had organised this anomaly scan because I knew something was wrong. I was far smaller in terms of a bump than I had been at this point in all three of my previous pregnancies. I still had not been recognised as pregnant at school, and the students are always the first to spot the good news. The most upsetting and noticeable difference was that I experienced very little movement from the baby, whereas I would have had plenty from far earlier on in previous pregnancies.

The consultant gave no diagnosis as to what was wrong, but I could for the first time see concern on his face. The baby appeared healthy but symmetrically small – the head, limbs and trunk were all in the correct ratios, only far smaller than they should have been. There was a further question mark over whether the baby had an echogenic bowel. This term is used when the baby's bowel appears brighter on the scan than would be expected, and, although it is not an indicator of any particular condition, it can indicate that there may be a genetic abnormality with the baby. It is not a reliable finding, however, as it can sometimes be due to the strength of the scanning machine, but it would be monitored in future scans. I remember asking whether the baby could have some form of dwarfism because it was so small, but the consultant advised me that it was far too early to be worrying about potential problems and that we should wait and see what the next scan would show. Again the consultant checked if there was any chance our dates were wrong, but I assured him they were not. We arranged another scan for the following week to see if there was any improvement and left the room shell-shocked.

Colin and I talked about nothing else in the following days. I trawled the internet for information on babies that were not growing well in the womb. The term that continued to emerge was IUGR, which stands for intrauterine growth retardation or restriction. It is diagnosed in babies that are failing to make their genetically predisposed size, beginning in the womb. In other words, some small babies are destined to be constitutionally small because genetically their parents are, but others fail to grow despite having the genetic material to do so. Therefore IUGR is a collective term for a multitude of reasons why babies might not grow well in the womb. These reasons can include the placenta not working properly or a genetic abnormality. Chronic hypertension or high blood pressure in the mother, or infection with certain pathogens in early pregnancy could also negatively affect growth. IUGR seemed to me to be pretty common, but seemed to be mainly diagnosed in women much further along in their pregnancies than I was, and the research was indicating that the earlier it is spotted, the more serious it is for the baby's outcome. The articles I found on the internet discussed early delivery, survival rates, premature labour, stillbirth and complications in terms of physical and intellectual development later in life. It was clear to me we were facing a serious health issue with our baby and that this pregnancy was going to be a long journey for all of us.

We arrived at our next scan and things were no better. The baby was now 6 oz (174 g), which was not sufficient growth since the last scan more than a week earlier. The consultant suggested we go for an amniocentesis within the next few days to try to get an idea of what was wrong with our baby. I remember the consultant explaining basic genetics to us, very well as it happened. He talked about the human genome being like a book with chapters. If there was a chapter missing (or presumably a whole unrequired extra chapter added), then the whole story was incomplete or didn't follow. This was a bit like a chromosomal problem. However, he went on to explain that that was not the full picture, as there could be words, lines or paragraphs missing or mixed up – which I imagined referred to individual gene or point mutations, as they are known. I let him explain away, without saying, 'Yes, I understand,' because he was doing such a good job of it, and I didn't want to be rude (even though I had been teaching senior biology, of which genetics was a huge part of the course, for nearly twenty years, and had covered genetics in detail in my degree in London). In any case, I was noting this great explanation, as it was a useful analogy to be subsequently used by me in classes. Later, we talked about Leaving Certificate biology and the textbook everyone used in the 1980s, and how we both loved the subject, although we were each now using it in very different ways.

It was at this scan that Colin and I also got some exciting news, although it was hard to celebrate, given the circumstances. The consultant asked us whether we would like to know the sex of our baby, as by now it was evident on the scan. For each of our pregnancies, I had wanted to know rather than wait for a surprise and this time was no different. I remember the consultant asking about the children we had already; when I said, 'Three boys', he said we would need to go shopping then. It was encouraging that, despite the emerging seriousness regarding our baby's growth, there was no suggestion of a negative outcome at this point, as we had no real information.

Although we smiled and put a brave face on things, the news that we were having a girl was completely overshadowed by the worry as to what might be wrong with her. We decided to call her Caroline that day, and it was nice to give her an identity, but I was so worried about her growth that I just could not relax and enjoy the moment. I had a day or two to prepare for the amniocentesis, and indeed for the results it might bring. I was worried about the potential abnormalities that Caroline might have, and at the same time terrified we might lose her due to the procedure, which really needed to be done now to see if we could shed any light on what was wrong with her.

4

TRYING TO ESTABLISH
A DIAGNOSIS

The amniocentesis procedure was not as bad as I had imagined it would be. The consultant and another doctor shared the procedure between them. The consultant located Caroline on the scan first and picked a spot near the placenta from which to take the fluid, so that if Caroline moved, she would not be pricked by the needle. He was able to keep an eye on her position at all times during the procedure. There was a slight delay in getting going, as Caroline started turning cartwheels and jumping all over the place. It was probably adrenaline from me giving her an energy surge, and we had to wait for her to settle down, which she did within minutes. The needle was inserted first through my outer abdomen, which was not too painful. Then the consultant asked the other doctor present to hold his arms for the next stage – which involved puncturing the tough muscle of the womb – because he did not want to end up pushing too far in or losing control of the sharp needle as he pushed firmly forward. This part of the procedure was quite uncomfortable for me. On the screen I could see the needle as it entered my womb and the space around Caroline. The consultant required considerable skill to manage scanning, watching and manoeuvring a needle simultaneously, even with a little help from the other doctor. An empty syringe was attached onto the end of the needle and a small amount of fluid was drawn and discarded to clean the syringe. A further twenty millilitres of fluid was drawn to be sent for analysis. The needle was carefully withdrawn and Caroline seemed unaffected by the invasion of her home. The needle had not touched Caroline and the fluid was clear, which was a good sign – no blood had been spilled. I breathed a sigh of relief as the sample was wrapped up to be sent to Britain for analysis.

I then went to the 'bloods room' – where blood tests are carried out – to have what is known as a TORCH test. This test involves a series of blood tests to check for some of the well-known serious infections that, if contracted during pregnancy, can damage a baby's growth and development. These infections include toxoplasmosis, rubella, cytomegalovirus and a few others, the first letters of all of them together spelling the word torch. The results of the TORCH test were also sent off to see if any answers could be found to illuminate why Caroline was not growing. By the end of the morning I was emotionally and physically drained. I experienced a few short cramps as I was warned I might, but took it easy for the rest of the day, and the cramps stopped within a few hours. I felt relieved the tests were being done to get answers but could not help feeling very sad that my baby and I were having to go through so much stress at a time that had been very happy for me in past pregnancies. All I could do at this point was hope the results would come back indicating we had no major chromosomal abnormalities or serious consequences of infection to contend with.

Having waited for what seemed like a lifetime, on edge all the time, Colin and I got a call from the consultant to say that the preliminary results were positive and that Caroline appeared not to have any major chromosomal abnormalities. The TORCH results were also good. We experienced a mixture of relief, on the one hand, coupled with intense worry and fear, on the other, as we still had absolutely no idea what was going on with Caroline. As far as I was concerned, the test had ruled out one set of issues, but I knew we still had a long way to go to get the answers we so desperately wanted.

The relief we had felt was temporary, as the next set of measurements indicated that Caroline was still not growing. A further two weeks had only yielded a 3-oz (75-g) growth to 9 oz (249 g). Caroline was now measuring a full six weeks behind the size she should have been for her gestation. At this point the consultant began doing Doppler checks on the umbilical artery leading from Caroline to the placenta. These checks were all done on the scanning machine: the artery would be located and the machine fixed on it for a few seconds to get a reading of the blood flow from me to Caroline via the placenta. Doppler checks can be very tricky to do if the baby is overly active, and Caroline just loved making things difficult by moving continually, making the location of the artery tough going. Any expectant mother who has Dopplers done becomes very familiar with the watery, gurgling noise the machine makes when it is recording the flow. The first time I watched the procedure, I was fascinated by the blue and red colours of the vessels and the blood flow, as well as by the unusual sounds, but as time progressed I grew to hate it all. The first time the consultant did the Doppler check, no issue appeared to emerge; however, the second time there was what is known as intermittently absent end-diastolic flow. The consultant described this to us in an easily understandable way. He explained that blood flow from the baby through the umbilical cord arteries should be like a tap that is on at a steady flow, but which is turned up in pulses continually. Between pulses there should still be a steady flow. In Caroline's case the pulses were there, but sometimes between them the steady flow would be absent as if the tap was being turned off between pulses. As this artery was a round-the-clock indicator of the circulation and health of Caroline, the check was at least indicating there were definitely physiological issues linked with the restricted growth she was suffering. The fact that this was recorded before the twenty-four-week mark was a source of great concern. Prolonged absent end-diastolic flow can become more serious quite quickly, making it necessary for the baby to be delivered immediately to avoid its being damaged by reversal of the flow, which can ultimately lead to serious illness or death.

The main issue with Caroline was that she was still at such an early stage of gestation, and measuring at an average of six weeks behind where she should have been, that delivery would cause her death anyway: she would simply be far too small to survive. If Caroline was to continue growing at the slow average growth rate of one or two ounces per week, she would run out of weeks of gestation and still be too small to get through birth and survive. Looking back over my diary, I see that I recorded that Caroline weighed only 4 oz (125 g) at twenty weeks, 6 oz (174 g) at twenty-two weeks, 9 oz (249 g) at twenty-four weeks and 10 oz (297 g) at twenty-six weeks. I took my diary along to every scan to record the measurements. Sometimes I would ask the consultant to print out the data for me from the measurements he took. He would measure the head circumference and other head measurements, the femur length in the leg, the humerus length in the arm, the abdomen circumference and then, using a formula called the Hadlock, would convert the measurements individually and collectively into a gestation equivalent. Sometimes all four measurements would combine to give the overall gestation and other times it would just be the head and abdomen. It was confusing, because if the head was included in the calculations, the gestation always came out better, as Caroline's head was marginally larger than the rest of her body. If the femur was included, however, it lowered the result. Of course, I used to readjust the figures with the head always included, so things did not seem as bad as they actually were. I would plot all the results on a graph at home to see the growth. What was encouraging for me was that there was always some growth, and the graph was slowly climbing. It just needed to climb a lot more quickly.

I found out that the fact that Caroline's head was growing out of proportion with her body and limbs was because of a phenomenon called brain sparing: the available food and oxygen are disproportionately diverted to the head, essentially to save the brain from damage. The limbs and abdomen suffer at the expense of the brain in dire circumstances. What was terrifying, however, was that all of this was evident so early in the pregnancy; I could only imagine what damage was being done to Caroline in trying to sustain this level of stress in a place that was supposed to be a safe, warm and comfortable haven. My own blood pressure was high on a number of occasions during these weeks, which was an indicator of the immense stress I was under. I had until this time always had low blood pressure. I am the type of person who has to climb out of the bath slowly, and not jump out of bed (not that there was ever a huge risk on that score!), otherwise I will become dizzy. When David was delivered, I spent ages in the recovery room, as my blood pressure was very low and would not come back up. But here I was, for the first time ever, with readings I could barely recognise. I knew I had to try to calm down for my sake and the baby's, but that was easier said than done.

5

SEEING THE SPECIALISTS
AS THINGS GET WORSE

It was around this time that Colin and I were advised to see more specialist experts in foetal medicine to see if any further light could be shone on Caroline's case. We travelled one day to have a series of scans by a number of experts and, as before, they could detect nothing with regard to a specific diagnosis. Caroline was so active that particular day, it was as if she was literally giving everyone the run-around. These scans confirmed what we knew: that Caroline was a symmetrically small but otherwise well baby. The Doppler readings again showed increased resistance, specifically in the uterine arteries this time, but the resistance was not (in the view of the specialist) at a level that could have come near to causing the degree of growth restriction evident in Caroline's measurements. It was mainly for this reason that it was suggested that Caroline might have some sort of skeletal dysplasia. There didn't appear to be any significant physical evidence for this diagnosis other than Caroline's small size, so it really was only a possibility. A skeletal dysplasia is essentially a form of dwarfism where the bones are genetically unable to grow properly. It can include many other problems with the skeleton and development in general. There are many forms of dysplasia, some of which are fatal, but it was mentioned that, due to Caroline's high levels of activity in the womb, this was unlikely in her case. There was no suggestion of what sort of dysplasia she might have, except that it was not the relatively common one, achondroplasia, in the case of which the limbs are severely restricted but the head and abdomen are close to normal dimensions. This potential set of conditions had crossed my mind earlier, when the growth issues had first manifested. I had seen a programme on primordial dwarfism and had begun researching all forms of dwarfism.

At the end of the consultation we were given very bad news, as if hearing Caroline might have a dysplasia was not bad enough. It was explained that if the growth retardation was solely down to placental insufficiency, in other words the placenta failing to work properly, then it was estimated that our baby would not live for more than another three or four weeks; however, if the condition was a skeletal dysplasia combined with a placental issue, our baby might survive, but would be extremely small at birth and might subsequently only grow to a possible adult height of three or four feet. We were told there might also be other very significant problems evident only at birth. It was extremely distressing to hear these two devastating scenarios, which offered little hope of our daughter ever leading a normal life. What was striking was the lack of any positive scenario; I think it was on that day that the realisation dawned that nothing as severe as Caroline's growth restriction had been seen before with any semblance of a positive outcome. The specialists were shocked, and struggled to see any chance of our baby being born without a disability.

This news hit us very hard indeed. I felt literally shell-shocked, walking out. I could not speak for many minutes, and I panicked when I thought about how we would cope with either of the outcomes the specialists had suggested. I spent that evening in an internet café, looking up skeletal dysplasias and marking them off one by one as they threw up things – such as finger abnormalities, misshapen vertebrae, bowed bones, narrow rib cages – that should be clearly visible on an antenatal ultrasound but had never been visible in Caroline. There were virtually no dysplasias that fitted Caroline's gestational dimensions or bone appearance. In fact very few existed for relatively symmetrically small babies. Although Caroline's limbs had fallen behind, this did not seem to be at an extent sufficient to merit an asymmetrical dysplasia, although this was what was being considered. The most significant observation was that, for nearly all the dysplasias, movement was significantly reduced in the uterus. However, our problem with Caroline was stopping her jumping around. I was not convinced, but there appeared to be no alternative.

During that evening I focused mainly on skeletal dysplasias, where whole limbs are shorter than head or trunk measurements, because that was what was mentioned to us as an indicator of a possible bone problem: all four of Caroline's limbs were measuring somewhat smaller than the head and abdomen. I did check the specialists' report, and felt that the difference was not significant, and in continually reading articles on IUGR, I would find out that the limbs could be neglected for the more essential parts of the body to develop. I still was not convinced, but needed to read more to see what skeletal dysplasias came up under that broad heading. After all, I knew little about what was going on and knew I was not ever going to be able to be impartial about anything negative I was told. Indeed, I regularly found myself setting out to disprove anything negative − clearly this was the coping mechanism working for me at that time.

I came across four main dysplasias under the criteria I have mentioned above. The first was achondrogenesis. The incidence of this condition worldwide was 1 in 60,000, so it was quite uncommon. The femur length is significantly shorter in babies with this condition than our baby's femur was measuring at the same point in gestation. Other symptoms of achondrogenesis included a narrow chest, short ribs, inward-turning feet and enlarged abdomen. None of these symptoms were apparent on our scans. However, this dysplasia also included a small chin and prominent forehead, which, it could be argued, our baby had. On balance I ruled it out, however, as there just weren't enough of the main features present to include it. The second dysplasia I looked at was fibrochondrogenesis. Again, thin long clavicles and short elevated scapula were features, alongside dumb-bell-shaped long bones that would have been visible by now on the scans. To my knowledge there were no signs of these, so I ruled fibrochondrogenesis out. The third dysplasia was termed Kneist dysplasia. At a one in a million chance, it had bone symptoms such as barrel chest, short neck and a flattened spine. That was out too. The fourth was dyssegmental dysplasia, which was significantly associated with heart defects and disorganisation of the vertebral bodies, as well as small orbits, none of which were issues for us.

I looked at many more conditions, but one by one I dismissed them in my own mind. That would work temporarily, but invariably I would end up essentially back at square one, not knowing what was wrong if none of these conditions fitted. This was definitely taking its toll on my mental health. The less I was able to find out and the more I was reading, the more suspicious of the unknown I was becoming and I often wondered whether I could keep going with a positive outlook for much longer, with no idea of what was wrong and all sorts of potential nightmares coming into my mind.

The specialists' report did have some positives in it too, which Colin and I were unable to focus on at the time because of the poor prognosis we had. The following parts of the baby were observed to look completely normal: head, face, spine, neck, skin, chest, four chamber views of the heart and greater vessels, abdominal wall, gastrointestinal tract, kidneys and bladder (the brain was not examined). This was a lot of good news, in hindsight lost completely to us at the time. The report said that the uterine arteries were elevated, which presumably meant the pressure was high in them, indicating they were not healthy, but the umbilical artery showed positive end-diastolic flow, which was amazing because this had been the vessel indicating a problem before. It was clear that the snapshot pictures of our baby were not giving the full picture. The skeletal dysplasia was considered because the placenta did not appear to be in sufficiently bad shape to be causing the level of growth retardation being observed, yet in our own hospital, in previous scans, the umbilical artery had been a problem.

I wondered if the vessels were all intermittently showing varying degrees of faultiness, which were not being caught by ultrasound together at the same time. Maybe if they were, the placenta would have been deemed the main problem and all these skeletal and other scary potential problems could have been dropped. But they were there and causing us much anguish. I needed to prepare for the fact that, at best, it seemed like we were facing either the death of our baby or a child with a significant disability. I felt as if I couldn't take much more stress and wondered how Caroline was surviving at all, with weeks on end now of corticosteroid hormones – released by the body during periods of stress and damaging to it if released over long periods – coursing through my veins and subsequently hers.

Colin and I stayed up all night after our visit to the specialists, discussing everything at length. Neither of us ate; we bought a pizza and left it in the box. It was a very close time for us both, however, and we really united. I talked of how terrified I was of delivering a dead baby, and he talked about how hard it would be if Caroline only reached three feet as an adult. We really mourned the chance she might never get a job, marry, or be able to enjoy many of the things the boys did. We worried about the prejudices or discrimination she might face, and the lack of facilities for many individuals with special needs. We wondered if she would be teased or laughed at, whether she would look different facially. We really went over everything, but deep down I knew I had seen the scans and that Caroline looked just small – nothing else, just small. She could have been any of my other children, but just smaller than she should have been. I knew our consultant was excellent at scanning, and despite the specialists' opinion, I felt he would have spotted a characteristic indicator of a dysplasia. Of course, this could certainly have been wishful thinking combined with a hefty dose of denial on my part, or maybe it was a maternal instinct, but I was not convinced of the possible diagnosis. It wasn't fitting the jigsaw for me.

To this day I just do not know why, but I believed Caroline's problems were due far more to my placenta being faulty than anything else, and I did mention this regularly, whenever we met new medical staff. The extent of the IUGR, and its severity, were negating this as a possibility on its own, but I kept thinking, 'Who knows how bad a placenta can be from the outside? Yes, this is very severe growth restriction, but where do you draw the line and say it cannot possibly be only the placenta.'

At this point we were not aware of other genetic glitches that could be responsible for poor growth in the womb. I can't help but wonder if there wouldn't be a benefit in a greater team approach to difficult pregnancies. We saw many obstetricians, but perhaps a geneticist could also have a role antenatally, looking at IUGR babies prior to birth. With the advent of 4D scanning – the most detailed scan available, offering a more photographic, clear image of the developing baby in the womb – geneticists may be able to assist with visual elimination of some conditions, particularly dysplasias. I know resources are tight, however, and this may preclude such an approach. All we could do was wait and see what would happen and hope beyond hope that things would not end up as badly as had been predicted at this appointment. During all of this stress, our consultant was at the end of the phone if we needed him, and that support was invaluable to us at the time.

The next morning, armed with a load of questions in true Hamilton style, Colin rang to see if we could meet the specialists again to talk the whole thing over. Very kindly, one of them was available and agreed to answer our queries. Colin agreed to go armed with a list of questions; I was too mentally and physically shattered.

Our first question was: if the baby dies will we have to have a funeral? I don't know if this was an indication of my hope beginning to fade, but I had remembered a baby funeral I had been at in the previous year and I knew I could not do that. The answer was that it would be our decision, and the hospital would take care of the remains if we wanted that. A post-mortem was advised if our baby died, to try to establish a cause, so that for any possible future pregnancy we would know if there was a genetic or familial problem.

Our second question was: is there any chance that there will not be a skeletal dysplasia? This question stemmed from the research I had done and from an attempt to hold on to some semblance of hope, I suppose. The answer was that there were no definites with our case, but that our baby did look as if it had a combination of skeletal and placental issues. There had been a mention of a slightly unusual head shape, although this wasn't mentioned in writing in the report.

This gave rise to our third question: what is the shape termed and what issues might it indicate? The answer was that our baby's head had a look of Edwards' syndrome, which we knew was a very serious chromosomal condition, but the head was not a clover shape (common in bone dysplasias) which is associated with early bone fusion. There was no evidence of early bone fusion on any of the scans to date. So again there were no definites, just the fact that our baby had a marginal head misshape.

The fourth question was: will the short stature suffered as a side effect of a dysplasia leave the baby in proportion skeletally, and what maximum adult height might be reached? The answer was that, at a best guess, the height would be between three and four feet, with relatively normal proportions.

We understood the difficulty this doctor must have had being faced with questions no one could really answer until after birth, but she did her best to give her opinion, which we asked for, honestly and professionally. We put many other questions to her. We asked whether the cause of the growth restriction might be metabolic (linked with chemical reactions in the cells or enzyme related) or endocrine (hormone related), rather than a dysplasia. The answer was that this was possible, but tests for it would have to be carried out after the baby was born. We asked again about the chances of survival, even though this had been made clear the previous day. I suppose we were hoping it wouldn't sound as bad or be as shocking the second time around. The answer was that if there was a skeletal dysplasia the chances of survival, albeit with disability, were reasonable to good, but with only placental insufficiency the chances were 'none'. It was reiterated that our baby might have only three to four weeks at current standings. We also asked what the chances of mental retardation were. The answer was that these were not definite, but that there could be possible mental developmental issues alongside other issues related to undersize evident at birth. We asked, too, about our baby's chances of ever living independently. The answer was that, depending on the dysplasia, living independently was possible as was a normal lifespan, but, again, if the problem was only with the placenta, our baby was unlikely to survive birth.

After this we enquired about support groups. The doctor said that she thought there were some, but not in Ireland, so we would need to have a look online. We asked about whether adoption agencies would consider a disabled child, if we felt we could not cope. She answered that this was not her field, and that we would have to contact the social welfare department. I know this question about adoption must seem like a callous and uncaring one, but we were terrified and we did not know if we would have the skills to cope with disability. We really didn't want to face this possible lifelong burden, as it seemed at the time. We were happy with our life and feared the impact a disabled child might have on our freedom to give all our children a good life. Of course, we see people who manage very well with disability, but we were not those people. They were the amazing people that we were not (in our own minds) at the time. I feel a bit ashamed of this reaction now, as it seems almost prejudiced, which it wasn't – we were just very frightened of the unknown and needed to talk about every option.

Of course, I had asked Colin to find out what could have caused this problem with the baby. I knew well the answer to this one, but psychologically I needed to hear it again from an expert, officially. It was a case of genetic bad luck; nothing we could have done would have caused or prevented it. I rephrased the question for Colin to ask again: is there any chance it might just be placental insufficiency causing the problem? In answering, the doctor reiterated that it looked like part of the problem, but it was not the only issue. We asked whether the echogenic bowel that had been noticed many weeks before was visible this time around, and the doctor answered that she could not see it, but again it depended on the machine and human interpretation of the image. She emphasised that with that particular issue you could ask ten doctors and get ten different answers. We asked if the placental insufficiency could be linked to the possible gene abnormality or whether it was entirely separate. It was clear they could be linked, and I had an idea of this because the placenta is the only animal organ comprised of maternal uterine and embryonic tissues. We asked whether the baby could end up wheelchair bound. The doctor answered that this would not necessarily be the case, and that the person could just be very small. Our final question was: what estimated birth weight can we expect? The answer was that we could expect approximately 3 lb 4 oz (1.5 kg) if delivered at thirty-six weeks and a maximum of 4 lb 8 oz (2 kg) if delivered at full term.

That was it: we now had the answers to all our questions. We did appreciate the opinion of the specialists, but it didn't make for very positive listening and didn't yield the positive outlook that we were hoping beyond hope it would.

6

KINDNESS AND CRUELTY

There were many occasions where the kindness shown to Colin and myself was exceptional. It might be the offer of a quiet room to wait in when we came to the hospital, or a kind word from a receptionist who had recognised that we were appearing for scans and tests far too often for things to be okay with the pregnancy. To be fair, there were few instances of insensitivity throughout the whole pregnancy, and we were very well looked after on the whole. One incident did upset me deeply. It occurred while our own consultant was on holiday, but we still had to go for a routine scan to check Dopplers and weights and measures to see how Caroline was doing. It was directly after we had heard the bad news from the specialists, and we were terrified that Caroline might die. We were also emotionally drained from the stress and worry the potential diagnosis was causing.

Because our consultant was away, the sonographer on

duty was asked to do our scan. Having arrived in the scan room, we gave a brief explanation of our case, mentioning that Caroline's survival was questionable and that things were not going well in terms of the possible dysplasia and growth generally. The sonographer did not seem very happy to be doing the scan; she looked quite cross and barely acknowledged what we were saying. At one stage during the scan Colin asked a question as much out of curiosity as an attempt to break the very awkward silence that was developing in the room. I found myself holding my breath as the atmosphere was palpably tense. The sonographer answered quite sharply, in our view, that she could give us no information. We said that was fine, and she continued while we waited in silence. I felt like an inanimate object just flopped on the bed, to be tested and prodded. I was starting to feel frustrated at, I suppose, being ignored while the scan was done. To be fair, the sonographer was probably concentrating, but we were used to being included in the process and free to discuss the images and ask questions. I do understand that we were not this person's patients and that she was possibly wary of discussing too much, but she was clearly not happy with something.

After a few minutes checking Caroline, the sonographer said a consultant should be doing the scan and she was not willing to continue. I am not sure if she knew how small Caroline was, or whether the Dopplers looked particularly bad. I could feel my blood pressure rising because I was worried something serious was happening. The sonographer said we should see the consultant on duty, which we said would be fine, and we asked when this would be as we would need to try to make further child-minding arrangements, given that we were only supposed to be in and out for a routine scan. At this point she got a little defensive in her tone and informed us, somewhat unnecessarily we felt, that we were in a hospital, that emergencies would precede us, that the consultant on duty might not see us, and if he did he would be doing us a big favour.

The attitude of this professional, combined with the constant stress I was under, left me in tears. When she noticed this, she told me there was no need to be getting upset. I had only asked for an idea of a time we might be seeing the consultant so we would have been able to make arrangements. I had three other children to look after, who were being minded by my parents, who might not have been in a position to stay on. I felt I was being done a favour by the system, the consultant who might see us and the sonographer we were annoying with our less-than-straightforward case. I was made to feel as though the hospital staff were choosing to help me, rather than that it was their duty to do so. Of course, I wished I was not there at all – I was beginning to dread the place.

One thing is for sure: that day, that woman got off very

lightly. Had it not been for the fact that I was emotionally drained and could not put up a fight for myself and Caroline, and tell the sonographer how horrible her attitude was towards us, she would have been put in her place, and deservedly so. It was hard to experience this stress on top of everything we were facing already. I know we all have off days, but this individual made a difficult time for us even more difficult, and that is hard to forgive. I do also appreciate that we were probably ultra-sensitive to negativity of any sort at that time, and that now we really must put the incident aside. I have no doubt that this individual is great technically with ultrasound equipment. But sonographers carry out scans at very special, poignant and sometimes tragic times of women's pregnancies and lives, and it is worth remembering that excellent interpersonal skills are as integral as technical expertise is to their job.

7

THE VERY DARKEST
OF DAYS

How do you ask someone to loan you the money to terminate a pregnancy? This is what Colin and I felt we had to do at one low point in the midst of all the drama, because Caroline's condition seemed to be so serious and we had no definite answers as to what was wrong with her. It was extremely frightening to see the look of anxiety on our consultant's face every time he took her measurements. Even though test results had come back indicating no major chromosomal abnormalities, this was no consolation really, because Caroline's growth was continuing to worsen significantly on every scan and no one had a confirmed reason for this. I was also looking up further information on the internet for up to six hours a day, and this was making matters worse: not only did the internet articles provide no answers, but the information was real worst-case-scenario stuff. It was startling how few positive-outcome stories there were with regard to babies with severe IUGR. I read about the disadvantage of short stature socially, psychologically, emotionally and physically. I found out about the incidence of special-educational-needs requirements for babies born at low weights. Mental retardation was likely according to some articles, and it was unfortunate that because I had a biology degree I could fully understand a huge amount of what I was reading.

Again, it has to be said that the consultant never once predicted the gloom-and-doom scenarios I was reading about – other than through the sometimes anxious look on his face (which I was becoming adept at reading) and his occasional mention that Caroline could die in the womb at any time as we had no clear diagnosis for her. He reiterated that Caroline was not behaving like a very sick baby would, appearing relatively happy and active, just very, very small. This was a constant source of comfort, as I imagined her as having energy and playing happily in the comfort of the womb as opposed to being starved of food and oxygen, which the medical information on her development was indicating. Of course, we will never know how Caroline felt at that time and whether hunger or pain were issues for her. It is hard to explain the feelings of intense guilt and low self-worth that would develop when I felt I couldn't even protect my unborn child within my body, and that a faulty placenta grown with mother and embryo cells was starving my baby.

Having three healthy children already made it harder for us to cope with. We had a perfect family and we did not want that to change. Our other children would invariably miss out on our time and attention if a disabled sibling was born.

So many questions arose in our minds. We have one income; how will we cope financially if Caroline has a serious lifelong condition? (Ireland does not provide adequately, in my view, for those with special needs.) Who will mind our other children if Caroline needs to spend lengthy spells in hospital? What about our plans to enjoy our retirement together after spending many years focusing on child-rearing? Will Caroline have pain, be ridiculed, or have a chance of a real life of her own? These and many other questions permeated our thoughts for weeks before we came to the conclusion that it might be better for everyone if we simply turned the clocks back and if I wasn't pregnant any more. That was how I dealt with the decision: I just would not be pregnant any more and then the intolerable pain, stress, guilt and mental torture would end.

The experience of that time really was like torture, as I rarely had longer than a minute or two – day or night – when I was not discussing, contemplating, researching, or dreaming, hoping or guessing about Caroline and her development. Colin and I discussed nothing else. I pretended I was listening to my other children, but I could not hear them because they were okay and Caroline was not. Of course, she was alive in me and her movements and hiccups were frequent physical reminders of her tiny fragile life growing far too slowly inside me. I had had enough of the worry and fear, and I wanted my life with my existing family back.

I had my story all planned out. We would be gone to wherever for further tests and I would have a miscarriage. There would be no funeral, as the hospital would take care of the remains. Things would be tough for a while, but then it would all be pushed to the back of my mind and I would miss Caroline but would have my boys back again and I would never get pregnant again. Of that I was sure. There was little doubt in my mind at this point that having made the decision I would follow it through, as I have always been extremely decisive and had managed to convince myself that the only option to save our lives, as we knew them, meant letting go of Caroline. It was excruciatingly painful but the unknown alternative was potentially worse. Colin was of a similar mind but also struggling, and I would often catch him deep in thought with a look of anguish and tears rolling down his face.

Online, I researched clinics all over Europe. I read all the details and shuddered when I discovered that because

Caroline's gestation was over eighteen weeks, she would have to be delivered surgically. I would have a general anaesthetic and be given drugs to dilate my cervix, and Caroline would be surgically removed by suction. At this point I deliberately did not seek out detailed information on exactly what happened at the suction stage, but had I done so, there would have been no question of going any further. I pretended to myself that the procedure would be gentle and almost peaceful for Caroline and that she would not have any sensations or fear, but I mainly focused on the feeling of being with my other children and happy and calm again with no worry or pain. Since then, to my horror, I have read and watched online the grim reality of what surgical abortion involves. The only advice I can give anyone in a similar situation is to be clear beforehand on what happens, because finding out afterwards is too late and must be psychologically crippling for the individual to deal with in hindsight.

We had made the decision. Everything was booked. There was, quite correctly in my view, no attempt to talk it through or change our minds by family: it was our decision, it was our nightmare, and only Colin and I could determine the outcome.

I woke early on the day we were to travel to the clinic. I can say with certainty that I was numb, as I recall little or nothing of the morning or the journey to the airport.

My earliest memories of the day were imagining as I checked in that I had 'murderer' printed on all my clothes. My worries were of a more practical nature: that the plane might be delayed and that I would miss my appointment, which had now become a symbol of freedom from torment, a release from captivity. I was pushing any thoughts of an emotional nature firmly to the back of my mind and being as pragmatic as I could be so as to mechanise the process as much as possible. It was only when the plane began to back out of its parking bay that the tears started to flow down my face. I turned to Colin and told him we would have to get a second opinion on the severity of Caroline's condition and try to get an answer as to why she was not growing. I felt she deserved this last chance – maybe, just maybe, somewhere as cosmopolitan as where we were off to would have experienced obstetricians who would have seen similar cases with positive outcomes. All I needed to hear was an expert say that he or she had seen a similarly growth-retarded baby do well without major disability. We were more than willing to have a baby with problems, just as long as the problems were manageable and not so debilitating as to cause major quality-of-life issues. Colin agreed, and the plan was to get to the abortion clinic where I was to have a scan to check dates and also a blood test and to talk about the procedure, which was planned to take place the following day. That left the afternoon of the first day to find a doctor somewhere who could tell us what was wrong. I felt a flicker of hope that we would get good news, just as I did every time we went for a scan or got results back. Where none of those had proved hopeful, for some reason I felt sure this attempt would be successful and I would be freed from the reality of terminating my little baby's life.

On the flight my mind began to wander inside the abortion clinic's doors. Although I could imagine little of the interior, I kept getting a flash image in my mind over and over again, and to this day I have no idea where it came from. I kept seeing a surgeon with masked face and long blue plastic gloves, not creamy white ones like those you would normally see. My eye would trace from his face to the top of his gloves at the elbow, and then slowly pan down to his fingers, where he would be holding an intact blood-smeared foetus in his blue hands. I could not see a face or hear a sound from the baby, but just as I looked for a detail to focus on, the surgeon would promptly drop the baby with a thud into a metal wastepaper bin lined with a similar blue plastic bag. Then another figure would quickly tie up the bag and whisk it away. In my head I would scream irrationally to stop them tying the bag as the baby would not be able to breathe, or sometimes before the surgeon dropped the baby in the bin, I would shout at him to be gentler so as not to hurt the child. It never really registered with me that the baby would already be dead, and I do not know what the blue plastic bin and gloves symbolised. I just knew that care for the baby after the procedure was important to me, and the idea of the baby just being rubbish to be discarded was hugely disturbing. I have, of course, no actual idea what happens to aborted remains or how they are treated, but this memory reminds me that I had little idea at the time of the violence of a suction abortion and how the image of an intact serene baby was far from the reality.

The remainder of the plane journey passed with my feeling intermittent spells of hopefulness, and having completed all the formalities, we emerged into the warm sunshine but with very heavy hearts. We travelled to the town the clinic was in and went for a coffee, as we were early for the appointment. I had avoided drinking coffee for the whole pregnancy so far, but then I had this one, almost as if in my mind the pregnancy was about to end anyway and there was no point being really health conscious if there was soon to be no baby. In my mind I was constantly switching from the hopefulness of good news from an, as yet, unidentified doctor somewhere, and the grim reality that time was running out and it was more likely the abortion would happen. We walked to the clinic through a leafy suburb of the town. I discussed with Colin whether there might be protesters outside, as I had heard this was a common occurrence at such clinics. The clinic was nestled among a row of buildings, relatively unrecognisable but for a small sign at the entrance. It was smaller and less clinical-looking than I imagined. There were no protesters outside. I took a deep breath as I approached the front door.

Once we had registered, we were asked to go to a waiting room to be called. This place seemed a bit surreal. For a start we were shocked that there were no men at all except Colin, who understandably felt very awkward. There were about fifteen women there, some visibly pregnant others not, some with a friend or mother, others on their own, some looking sombre and others chatting without an apparent care in the world. I felt awful, as though I had joined some group of like-minded women – only I was not one of them, I wasn't supposed to be there. I had not travelled there because I had an unwanted pregnancy or made a mistake or changed my mind. I wanted this baby more than anything; I had been elated when I discovered I was pregnant, even more so when I had found out I was having a girl. It dawned on me that I was there because I was terrified of the unknown and was selfish about accepting the potential life changes Caroline would bring to our family and happy lives. I felt lonely, trapped, depressed, guilty and scared – all the emotions this abortion was supposed to put an end to. I think at this point I was going through the motions, but the seeds of doubt that this abortion would serve to fix anything had now been firmly sown. I said nothing to Colin as I waited for my name to be called.

I entered a tiny room where Caroline was scanned. I was ready to be asked why I was having a termination. I had a paltry answer prepared: that we had three children already and were not in a position to have a fourth. It sounded ludicrous really, but I didn't want to tell the whole story about Caroline and how she wasn't growing well in the womb and that doctors had found nothing really wrong but that we just weren't keen on taking any chances. Let's face it: that would have sounded even more paltry. However, I do not recall actually ever being asked why we had made the choice. I vaguely remember receiving, as I had blood taken, a superficial, glancing description of what was to happen the next day. It sounded quick and easy, with some pain but nothing that could not be managed. I had to pay a considerable sum of money at this point in cash as a deposit to keep my place, as if it were a theatre booking of a more social kind, and I was advised to go to a pharmacy and buy some maternity towels and strong painkillers. The matter-of-factness of it all was a bit disturbing, but it was the business of this private clinic. It was what happened every day, but not to me of course. I am glad now for the cold approach because it almost shook me back to reality. If people had been extra kind and sympathetic I might have wanted – in some sick way – not to let them down by pulling out, or perhaps I would have had that warm fuzzy feeling I get when people are nice to me, inferring what I am doing is right, when for me personally, it or I would never have been right.

I proceeded to the pharmacy, but despaired as I picked up maternity towels – the last time I had bought them I was excited about the birth of my last son, Samuel, and for me they were a symbol of the rite of passage birth brings in giving life, not mopping up death. I also felt like throwing the pain relief back onto its shelf, because if I was going to do this to my daughter I deserved all the physical pain as a reminder of how weak and selfish I was being. Yet I still proceeded to the checkout and bought the lot. I was angry at this point; I felt it was unfair that I had all this to go through, in addition to the pregnancy and stress. I was full of regret for not stopping at baby number three instead of going for a fourth. However, I reminded myself we had the afternoon to try to get some answers.

We were due to stay two nights and decided to book into our guest house – one recommended by the clinic – before going in search of answers. The guest house was a few miles from the clinic. It was an old three-storey house complete with big windows and a narrow path running up to the front door. It was not a walk-in sort of place, so we rang the bell and waited. A small Korean man promptly answered the door. We said who we were and followed him to a little kitchenette, where his extended family was gathered chatting and having tea. I felt them glance at me briefly and knowingly, but they were all smiling and friendly. The place was not at all like an official guest house with a payment area or foyer or sitting room; there was just this area where the family were and the stairs to the rooms. The man asked for payment in cash for the two nights, which I found most irregular, given the normal procedure of paying on departure. This was no normal guesthouse, however, as I was to find out. I asked to see the room first, as I was nervous about this upfront payment and being given a hovel-like room. The room was tucked away up near the attic and, in fact, we found it fine, so Colin paid the man and we sat down to have a look around it. The first strange thing was that the breakfast was already there, ready on a tray, and the room had a fridge containing milk and fruit juice for the two mornings. It was clear there would be no 'going down to breakfast' here, which of course made perfect but disturbing sense, as this was the pre- and post-abortion accommodation. It was a private recovery room with food and drink, a television and an accompanying bathroom. It was designed for guests who would be staying put, not exploring the local area.

Being in this room brought the shocking reality to bear again: I was here to have a pregnancy termination, and when I returned to this room the following day my baby would be dead. I felt real despair as I flopped onto the bed. I shuddered as I imagined all the women who had felt that same despair and who had probably cried themselves to sleep out of pain and sadness, perhaps mixed in some way with relief. As I sat quietly, something urged me to pull the duvet and the sheet back and look at the mattress. I saw what I had known I would see: many light-brown, faded bloodstains. This was the abortion house, where women arrived and bled the last of their pregnancy into this bed, where, although cleaned, the mattress still bore the evidence of their actions. I was to join this group of women within twenty-four hours. I cried while Colin held me tightly, telling me it would be all over soon and that everything would be okay.

Within an hour of arriving at the guest house, we set off to find a doctor who could scan me and give us the good news that this was all a big mistake and would assure us that Caroline would be fine and would catch up in size during the second half of the pregnancy. Stupidly, in the stress of organising the visit, we did not organise for our mobile phones to allow roaming calls, so Colin – armed with a phone directory – set about ringing all the major hospitals in the area from a public phone booth with blaring traffic passing by. Looking back, we can smile now at Colin's attempts to work out what the receptionists were saying, both due to the background noise and the varying accents – ranging from Asian to African to indigenous – he encountered. I could read his lips spelling addresses and numbers back to them, saying 'B for bravo' or 'F for foxtrot' to busy and frustrated staff who were wondering what we thought we were doing trying to get an appointment with an expert obstetrician for that same day. Looking back, it was ludicrous, but it was a last-ditch attempt by us literally to save Caroline from ourselves. Unbelievably we got the number of a private clinic where we managed to get a scan appointment for seven o'clock that evening. This place, we were told, was the best.

We arrived exhausted and hot after walking miles, as we had got off at the wrong station and it was still very warm outside. We entered a very plush waiting area complete with tea, coffee, sweets, bottled water, books and very comfy sofas. We tried to explain that we needed to see the top obstetrician, whose name we had been given, because our case was very severe and we were only in this country for a few days. The receptionist told us to our disappointment that the person we wanted to see was not on duty that evening and that she could arrange for us to see him two days later. I wanted to scream with frustration, because this particular man was the expert I wanted to see; I had come across his name on many of the articles I had read online over the previous months and I had seen him on television discussing foetal medicine. I had a massive dilemma because I had no arrangements in place to stay away for longer, my appointment at the abortion clinic was the next day, and our flights were booked for the following day; cancelling and rearranging everything again meant taking the chance there would not be another appointment option at the clinic. The receptionist offered to have Caroline scanned by one of the expert research fellows who would have been very experienced but probably no more so than consultants we had seen in Ireland. We spoke to a lovely woman, who listened to our story and admitted most honestly when she heard the most recent growth measurements that our case would be beyond her level of expertise and such a scan would essentially be a waste of our money, as nothing new was likely to be gleaned by her. Oblivious to the plans we had made for the following day, of course, she strongly advised we wait the few days to see the main specialist.

We spoke little as we boarded a train to return to the guest house. I sat and watched professionals, tired-eyed after a day's work, typing away on their laptops. I watched mothers sit with shopping in one hand, the other holding their child's hand. I remember sitting and thinking to myself about what I would do. After a few minutes contemplating the options, which were poor in my eyes at the time, I was suddenly aware that Caroline had started to dance. I had not been aware of her movements for a few days – I suppose I was trying not to be – but there was no way I could ignore this. In the still of the carriage Caroline was vigorously turning somersaults and sticking a tiny arm or leg right into my solar plexus. I am not a particularly spiritual person and could easily explain this as being due to my finally resting and relaxing, enabling Caroline to wake up and make her presence known. I believed, however, that it was her telling me she was with me, alive and well enough to give me a good old poke. I believed it was her call for survival, a final reminder she was my daughter, a part of me I should not give up on. I couldn't stop the tears flowing again on that train, but this time they were not tears of sadness but of relief that Caroline had finally helped me find the courage to give birth to her, however ill she might be. She gave me the hope that it would be better than predicted. I felt huge and immediate relief that I would not have to return to the clinic, with its oppressive atmosphere of fear and trepidation. The only thing I had to do now was tell Colin that I couldn't go through with it after all and convince him that we would manage, however things turned out.

I said nothing until we got up to the room and then blurted out that I could not do it. Of course this was a shock to him, and he did speak to me about why we had decided to come here in the first place and that if we stopped now there would be no going back. It took a while, but eventually Colin recognised from the look on my face that I would not be terminating the pregnancy – I suppose, having been my partner for fourteen years, he knew that 'not for changing' look. I remember him smiling and saying that, whatever we were to face, we would do it together and we would get through it all somehow. I could tell he meant that, but I had to keep asking him if he was sure, because although it was ultimately my decision, I knew that if Caroline ended up being very sick we would both fare better if we were together on the decision to keep going with the pregnancy.

Within seconds of making the decision we were both in hysterical tears and laughter at the same time. Afterwards we talked of a physical lifting sensation we felt over the minutes that followed. It was as if a great weight was literally lifted off us, which emotionally was the case. We had no idea how much stress we were under at that time, but, looking back, it is clear it was immense. Neither of us has ever felt such emotional upheaval since. The payment upfront for the procedure and the room made sense to us now: we were not the first couple, and would not be the last, to travel this lonely road, only to change our minds and take what was for us the right path to peace. We raced – running the whole way – to the nearest internet café and booked two seats to fly home the next morning. We did not sleep at all that night, partly because of the adrenaline coursing through our veins, and partly, in my case, because I was afraid of closing my eyes and letting in the nightmares about the nights other women had spent in the same bed. Colin rang the clinic early the next morning and we filed out of the room and house without as much as a glancing look back. On the train to the airport Colin rang his mother to tell her we were keeping

Caroline. There was silence, which we misconstrued for a split second as regret, until we realised we were hearing her strained, choked voice through tears, saying, 'You have done the right thing.' She was never going to say to us beforehand not to go ahead, but she knew us well enough to know we wouldn't ever have got over it if we had.

The plane journey back couldn't have been more different from the one going out. We chatted about how much we wanted to see our other children. We had a positive attitude towards facing whatever would come. We both knew we had had a very near miss. I realised that if I had gone through with the termination I could never have lived with the guilt. I would have spent the rest of my life wondering if Caroline would have been healthy aside from her growth issues. I could never have reconciled my rationale for doing it with my conscience, and I think it would possibly have ruined Colin, me, and our family far more than facing a potentially disabled child together. I learned how difficult a decision an abortion is for any woman to make, that it is fuelled by fear of the unknown and a change in life that for many is unwelcome in their circumstances. I could never judge a couple or a woman who makes the choice to end a pregnancy. I am just glad I changed my mind, or Caroline did it for me. Having been exhausted for what seemed like months I was exhilarated, full of determination and convinced that everything would be fine.

Of course, we had no idea this exhilaration would be short-lived and that we were only just over halfway on our pregnancy journey, with many more mountains to climb in the weeks to come. Nevertheless nothing could have been worse than those few torturous days. I was not afraid anymore. I had accepted that however Caroline would be I would love her and look after her. I had been to hell and back, and I was stronger for it.

8

CAROLINE'S SLOW FIGHT FOR SURVIVAL

Our decision to go on with the pregnancy was a turning point for both of us. Although growth remained slow for a good number of weeks, there were continual steps towards a viable birth weight: 9 oz (249 g) at twenty-four weeks went to 10 oz (297 g) at twenty-six weeks, which went to 12 oz (341 g) at twenty-seven weeks. At twenty-eight weeks there was what was for us a massive leap: to 1 lb 1 oz (472 g). This was still so far behind where Caroline was supposed to be that I think the consultant covering for our own was bemused by the palpable excitement we were exuding. But to us this was progress; Caroline was nearing that 1 lb 2 oz (500 g) mark that indicated a small chance of survival, despite all the odds and predictions of the specialists. She was still moving well and was showing no signs of dying without a fight. We were unaware at the time of the potentially serious consequences for her long-term health if she were to be born at or around this mark. We were far more positive and determined to be there for Caroline.

The end-diastolic flow was usually absent at her ultrasound scans and there was definite evidence of the redistribution of blood to the brain. Caroline was undoubtedly sacrificing development and growth of the abdomen and limbs for the protection of her brain. The replacement consultant, who would not have been as familiar with Caroline as our usual consultant, was visibly shocked by her condition and he agreed with the specialists we had consulted in that he too felt survival for Caroline was unlikely. He admitted very honestly that in his whole career as an obstetrician he had never seen a case so severe in terms of growth retardation. He did mention that he saw no signs whatsoever of a skeletal dysplasia, which encouraged me greatly, not because his remark ruled that out, but because it meant there was conflicting opinion on what was wrong with Caroline, which suggested no one really knew. If it were all conjecture, maybe, just maybe, Caroline would prove everyone wrong and be healthy. I had to try to ignore the potential prognoses now as it was clear Caroline's case was a unique mystery and only time would tell.

At twenty-nine weeks our usual consultant had returned. The weight was 1 lb 3 oz (536 g), so we felt steady progress was being made. All limb measurements were taken and the results clearly indicated again, as before, that the head of the baby was growing at a greater rate than the abdomen and limbs. The limbs and abdomen, however, were not more than a few days apart from each other, which made me question the comments in the specialists' report which had inferred a bigger difference between the limbs and the rest of the body. The baby's weight was now measuring that of a 23-week-old baby as opposed to a 29-week-old one. The Dopplers were showing the absent end-diastolic flow as usual. We discussed a plan of action on this visit because Caroline was now a potential survival case. We talked about aiming to get Caroline to 1 lb 10 oz (750 g), and then administering steroids to mature her lungs and deliver her early, rather than risk death in the uterus. The consultant also suggested we meet the paediatrician and hospital counsellor the following week to discuss our case and talk about the possible consequences for our baby. I mentioned reading that aspirin had been administered to some women with babies with severe IUGR. Although the results varied with regard to outcome, it was decided that there might be no harm in starting aspirin administration in the hope that it might increase blood flow to the baby by thinning the blood, and so assist oxygen and nutrients to get through to her.

At thirty weeks' growth the baby's weight was 1 lb 4 oz (579 g), which was disappointing as one ounce of growth in a week was not good. Our consultant reminded us that it was more helpful to examine growth trends over two-weekly periods, rather than weekly, and that ups as well as downs were to be expected over short periods of growth. I couldn't help but feel that he was just trying to make a bad situation better, but I had no choice but to accept his point.

We met with the counsellor and paediatrician, who listened together to our journey so far. We had an expectation that the paediatrician would tell us more about what Caroline's chances would be and what kind of problems we would have to be prepared for with her. However, both the counsellor and paediatrician seemed to be there mainly to listen to our understanding of what was happening. I wasn't sure, in hindsight, whether Caroline was expected to die at any time at this stage – we were at the three- or four-week point at which her demise was expected – or whether we were meeting specialist staff who might look after her when she arrived. Perhaps it was neither, just a meeting in case of either scenario. I found the counsellor very sympathetic and supportive. After we met her, she took to being present at the scans on occasion, and I am not sure to this day why. I did not want to ask why she was there, in case she was insulted and thought we minded, which we did not. I wondered whether she was curious to see this little baby, whose day-by-day defiance of scientific probabilities we had gathered by then, everyone was talking about. Sometimes I wondered whether the counsellor was asked in to verify that we were being told regularly that Caroline was in danger of dying in the womb at any time, as a sort of insurance in case we claimed we didn't know. We were adamant at this stage that this was not on the agenda, and perhaps this was rather disconcerting for a still gravely worried consultant.

The week following thirty weeks' growth presented another potential problem issue in that the fluid around the baby seemed to be on the generous side. I had noticed a big, quite rapid increase in the size of my bump, and friends and family were also commenting positively. Unfortunately it was not a good sign. When the fluid index was measured, it was twenty-four; excess fluid shows an index of twenty-five. This condition is known as polyhydramnios and can be linked with foetal abnormalities. It can also cause premature labour and placental abruption – detachment of the placenta from the uterus, a potentially serious condition because of a risk of haemorrhage. Here we were again with yet another worry and another set of enquiries to make on the internet. The risk of intrauterine death of the baby was reiterated during this week although the Dopplers were no worse than before. With ten weeks to go, at most, Caroline was still giving us cause for concern, ticking almost every scary box that could be ticked in any pregnancy. However, she was still alive, growing slowly and continuing to dance around regularly in her spacious womb.

On 18 July, when we reached thirty-one weeks, the fluid

index was above twenty-five, which was a worry, but it was still considered borderline high and so not an imminent cause for concern. The baby's weight was estimated to be 1 lb 9 oz (704 g), which was great growth relative to previous weeks, as could happen, as the consultant had pointed out. I was ecstatic at five ounces of new growth. I remembered back to Caroline's weight at nearly twenty weeks, which was only 4 oz (125 g); here she was now growing that much in a week. The Dopplers were no worse, and the plan remained to get to 1 lb 10 oz (750 g) and deliver after the administration of steroids to mature the lungs. The fact that femur length was falling behind other measurements was recorded in the notes, but again it was not actually any worse than abdomen growth, with both measuring twenty-four weeks as opposed to the real gestational age of thirty-one weeks.

At this stage Caroline was a full seven weeks' growth behind where she should have been for her gestational age. At our weekly appointment the consultant noticed that the baby's heart rate decelerated for a period during the ultrasound scan, and he decided it would be safer if I started to come into the hospital for biweekly traces of the baby's heart. These CTGs, as they were called, would indicate any problems with the baby's status and, now that we were at a survivable weight, might indicate the need for an immediate delivery if they showed any deterioration in the baby's health.

The CTGs involved attaching to my abdomen a band with

a round recording device capable of picking up a heartbeat. It recorded both the heart rate and movement, as I would press a button every time I felt Caroline move. I was familiar with these traces from previous pregnancies, as I had always been attached to one for a period of time in admissions before being admitted to an antenatal ward in readiness for delivery. It can be a positive experience to hear the baby's heartbeat chugging away, but obviously it makes it possible also to hear when things are not going well and the heart rate slows down. There are all sorts of tricks to keep the baby awake during the trace: drinking cold water helps the baby stay alert so that the device can record the required movements, but doing so can also be very uncomfortable, as before long the mother-to-be's bladder is full, and she can be dying to go to the toilet while waiting for the trace to be officially signed off. Caroline's traces were very different from those of my other babies. She had a less variable heart rate – the range of ups and downs recorded as a result of movement or anything else were less evident on Caroline's traces – and this seemed to be a problematic issue for the midwives at times. Her heart seemed less reactive, I suppose. The other significant problem was finding Caroline's heartbeat at all, as she was so small. Sometimes she would continually move, requiring the bands to be readjusted to her new heart position. Before long I was adept at sorting out the stoppages on the machine by relocating Caroline so that the data collection could continue.

A few days after the consultant had first suggested I have biweekly CTGs, I was having a trace done and was concerned with the level of foetal movements, so I had another scan to confirm that things were okay. At this point I was filling in a kick chart early because of Caroline's condition. Normally a pregnant woman would record her baby's movement from thirty-five weeks on a kick chart, counting ten kicks or movements per day, and if ten movements were recorded, she would continue the following day. If ten movements were not easily recorded, the procedure was to go into hospital for a check. I had to start doing this for Caroline at thirty weeks. It was an onerous task. Because she was so small, I sometimes found it hard to tell if it was actually her movement I was feeling. I was told to monitor her movement informally all day as well. This was exhausting and stressful, as I would constantly be on the alert, trying to sense her well-being, and I felt a huge pressure to keep focused on her. It was impossible to relax. I also felt worried that if I did not notice a problem and get to the hospital quickly enough and she died, it would be my fault.

I sometimes struggled to see an end to this pregnancy and, despite feeling positive as much as possible, there were times when I wondered if all the worry and stress would amount to nothing and if Caroline might die anyway. Those moments became fewer as time went on, however. I had to do what I had to do for Caroline. I felt very guilty about having even contemplated aborting her, and my tenacity about doing everything I had to do to the letter of the law was reciprocity for almost letting her down in the most awful way. The scan was fine, apart from generous fluid levels, which could have explained my not feeling as many movements, so Caroline was fine. Perhaps a little paranoia was beginning to set in with the constant worry surrounding this baby. One other query raised during this week was whether the baby's facial profile was unusual. I had myself noticed that her forehead seemed a little prominent and that the angle leading to the bridge of the nose was quite acute on the scans. It was debatable, but nonetheless, like the presence of an echogenic bowel, something that might have indicated a genetic problem.

At thirty-two weeks the baby weighed 1 lb 12 oz (784 g), which was encouraging. We had now passed the 1 lb 10 oz (750 g) target, but the consultant felt it would be rash to deliver when no deterioration seemed to be occurring: the baby was very active, the fluid index had dropped to a normal twenty-three again, and the Dopplers were unchanged. The consultant explained that our baby's condition was chronic, rather than acute, and that we would be giving the baby a much better chance of survival with fewer complications associated with prematurity if we were to sit tight and keep monitoring. He was due to go on holiday that week, so another consultant would be taking over again. We discussed my concern that if something were to go wrong at home, I wouldn't be able to detect it as the foetal movements were weak due to Caroline's size. Colin and I felt highly nervous about losing this baby when we had reached a relatively good weight. I asked whether I would be safer being monitored in hospital, but the consultant felt that being in hospital might lead one poor trace to cause a reaction that caused Caroline to be delivered in haste. I could appreciate this and had no wish to have the baby any earlier than was necessary, but I felt that the responsibility to have to make the call about reduced foetal movements was great. I asked whether the Dopplers could be done biweekly again for my own reassurance, which seemed a possibility, although for the following week that would be up to the other consultant looking after us. The baby's head shape was described at the scan this week as 'strawberry shape', yet another indicator that there might be a genetic issue with Caroline.

At this stage, Colin and I were wondering whether there was really any chance that Caroline could be born a normal, healthy baby, but we had to keep positive and remember that until we received an actual diagnosis, nothing was confirmed. Out of pure nervousness, we made an appointment to see our consultant before he went on holiday on the Friday of that week, to check that all was okay before he left. In hindsight, I feel we were being selfish: he must have been extremely busy with all his other patients before he left. He was doing everything he could and we were demanding more of his time. He never complained, although he must have been frustrated or even a little annoyed. I know I would have been, in his shoes, but he fitted us in and reassured us everything was as it had been days earlier. To me, this was an indication of the sheer generosity of the man. We parted company, and Colin and I thanked him for his help with our baby, as we did not expect to see him again over two weeks later; we felt sure there would be some change that would pre-empt a delivery. The last decision made that day was to increase the CTGs to every two days, which was a huge commitment and a strain for us as we tried to manage three children at home. Invariably the traces would take up a whole morning and were very stressful at times, but if that was what was needed, that was what we knew we had to do. Caroline's care had truly become a partnership: we were doing our bit and the consultant was doing his.

At thirty-three weeks we met the replacement consultant for our, by now, routine scan. He remembered seeing us previously, and I must admit I took a little pleasure in pointing out that our baby was still hanging in there. He seemed genuinely surprised. The weight was 1 lb 13 oz (825 g) and we were excited to be approaching the 2-lb mark. Foetal movement was good and fluid good. Again the head shape was queried, but was described by this consultant as being clover shape, which was a bit disconcerting as my research indicated that the two head shapes mentioned were not the same and indicated different potential abnormalities. It was slightly encouraging, however, as we did wonder if, since there was a discrepancy between two consultants about the head shape, perhaps it was not a clear-cut misshape. I remember our own consultant continually reiterating that ultrasound scanning was not an exact science. When he checked Caroline's head shape, he could show me the unusual shape, and then with the slightest movement of the transducer used during the ultrasound scanning, show a perfect head shape. It was clear that the scan image was truly in the eye of the beholder, and it was important to allow for differences in interpretation. Dopplers showed end-diastolic flow was absent but there didn't seem to be any redistribution to the baby's brain and we weren't sure whether this was encouraging or not. The consultant planned to see us the following week but explained that he would be 'very suspicious' about our baby having an abnormality due to her size. I interpreted this statement to mean that there was likely to be an abnormality with Caroline when she was born.

It is hard to put into words the constant ups and downs we felt during this time. Our minds were constantly going over the possible outcomes. Everything we did with the other children was almost like an act; it felt surreal. Nothing made us happy except when we imagined that things would be okay and our baby would survive and be healthy and happy. Then the crashing thoughts of the alternative outcome would force their way in and demolish the little hope we were trying to muster. The early pregnancy nausea had gone, but had been replaced with intermittent and sometimes severe waves of intense sickness and exhausting stress. We talked about nothing but the baby and almost destroyed ourselves trying to think of what had gone wrong. Having no answers was the hardest part, as we could not prepare for the unknown.

I have many clear memories of sources of great comfort throughout this time. One such source occurred when our consultant asked us what our two-year-old did when he was sick. We replied, 'Sleep and rest and look for comfort.' The consultant would then look at the ultrasound machine, which would show Caroline leaping about as usual, seemingly without a care in the world. There was clearly something wrong, but Caroline was not behaving as a sick baby would. She was active and comfortable. Moments of hope like this remain with me even today.

Around this time, the consultant enlightened us about his management philosophy for babies with potential problems. He believed in looking at the whole picture, the whole baby. In our case, as I mentioned earlier, he felt it was important not to deliver Caroline early just because she was not growing properly, when there was no acute problem.

I remember having numerous discussions or debates with him throughout this time. He would ask me what I thought would happen if we noticed Caroline had the cord around her neck. I said, 'Deliver.' He said that, no, he would not deliver; he would look at how the baby was behaving and if everything seemed okay, he would just monitor the situation. It seems babies have cords around their necks much more often than we mothers realise. From that day on I was straining to get a look at the scans, convinced that on top of everything else Caroline had the cord around her neck.

I am not sure if this is slight paranoia, but I am sure the scanning screen moved slowly throughout the pregnancy from fully within my view to an angle that made it trickier for me to see. If that was the case, I can fully appreciate why. There is no point in my denying that I was a real pain at times. I would spend hours researching on the internet and then come in armed to the hilt with queries, suggestions and all sorts of possible theories to shed light on what was happening to Caroline. Of course, this was my way of coping and I suppose feeling in some way partially in control of what was going on. I could tell the consultant wanted me to try to relax and to let him deal with all the medical stuff and the theorising. He implored me on more than one occasion to cut down on the researching. He could tell by my reaction and slight smile that that was unlikely to happen, so he asked Colin to intervene. Colin said nothing but gave him a look as if to say, 'Do you think I have any control over what this woman does?' The consultant would glance back in full comprehension of the silent communication that was taking place. I know I must have been frustrating to deal with – even annoying at times – but the consultant always dealt with us with patience, kindness and professionalism. That level of humanity and downright decency was invaluable to us. Of course the patience shown to us translated directly into his philosophy of observing and waiting for the best and right time to act in terms of delivering Caroline. We firmly believe that, in adhering to this approach, he was instrumental in avoiding potentially huge prematurity complications and life-changing problems for Caroline.

On Thursday 31 July I returned to the hospital to have a routine trace. I was at thirty-three weeks and two days gestation. The trace did not go well, as Caroline's heart rate was not reacting well to movement, the movement was not great, and, most importantly, the heart decelerated at one stage, which was a worrying development. That sound of our baby's rhythmical heart rate slowing right down to what seems like a standstill is a memory that strikes fear into me still when I think of it. Invariably it climbed slowly back up to normal and might have been just one of those things, but, of course, it could also indicate problems. Given Caroline's condition, it was a cause for concern. I was admitted to the hospital for observation and given two steroid injections, the purpose of which was to develop the baby's lungs in case a delivery was necessary. The plan from here until delivery was to have twice-daily CTGs and twice-weekly scans to monitor the baby's progress. If at any time the traces proved unreassuring, then our baby would be delivered by emergency Caesarean section.

At this point I was not sure whether I would simply stay in the hospital for a period of observation or whether I would be there until Caroline was delivered. I had very mixed feelings about the whole thing. On the one hand, being in hospital would allow me to offload some of the responsibility I was feeling when having to tune into Caroline's movements all day, and the worry when she had a sleep about whether she would wake up and start moving again. On the other hand, a long spell in a public antenatal ward, and the stress that would bring, played on my mind. It was going to be a very lonely time spending all day confined when I wasn't sick. It would leave me with a lot of time to fill and it was going to be hard not to spend that time thinking of all the different outcomes for Caroline. I was also concerned for Colin, as he would have to manage the three boys on his own with no help. Although I knew he would cope, having three boisterous boys twenty-four hours a day, seven days a week, without my help in the evenings and on weekends, was going to be a scenario very different to the usual one. He would also have to deal with the worry over me and Caroline and know that we would not have each other to talk to properly until the pregnancy was over. This made things even harder. Of course, family members offered their help, but they had their own families and lives to manage; essentially Colin would be managing a stressful situation and full-time childcare day and night entirely on his own for the first time for a prolonged period. I knew I would miss the boys an awful lot, and I felt they had been through a fair amount of stress themselves during the pregnancy as it was. I knew, however, that I would have to do what was right for Caroline and was resigned to staying put if that was the suggestion made at our next scan.

All went okay for the remainder of the week and we met the replacement consultant again on Monday 4 August. The baby's weight was approximately 1 lb 15 oz (860 g) now – very close to the 2-lb mark which sounded so much better than 1 lb something. Dopplers were unchanged, with mainly absent flow, and the fluid was fine. Thankfully the consultant decided to allow the pregnancy to continue, due to there being some growth and no deterioration. He told me to stop taking aspirin in case I needed to be delivered, due to an increased risk of haemorrhage.

It was at this meeting that I asked the consultant for his opinion on whether Caroline would survive the birth and how he felt she would be afterwards. He told us that the neonatal unit would certainly be able to keep her alive but

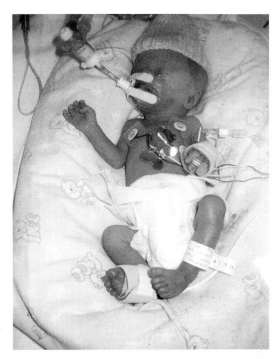

Caroline's first
hours of life in neo-
natal intensive care.

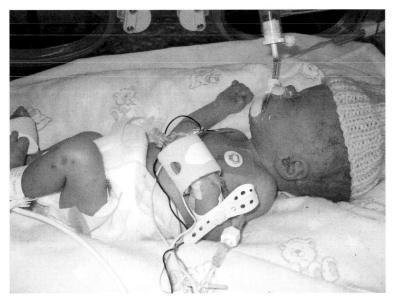

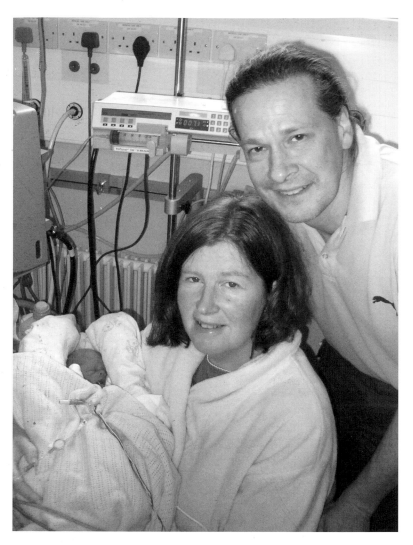

Relief and exhaustion – Caroline's first cuddle with Mum and Dad.

Right: Caroline's first outfit.

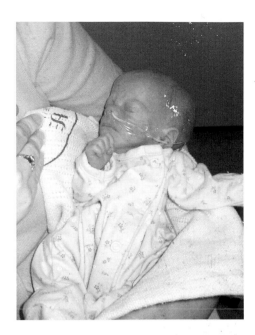

Below: Leaving the hospital at last with her proud brothers.

Exciting times at home.

Above: Where's
my rubber duck?

Right: Christmas
morning 2009.

Who needs a spoon when you have fingers?

Nothing beats a good book!

Right: Freezing at Fanore Beach, Summer 2010.

Below: Look how big I am! Summer 2011.

that he would not be overly hopeful about how she might be on her first birthday. I felt there was an 'if she even makes it that far' bit left out, and again I felt a chill of fear up my spine at the thought. I was not cross at the response, as I had asked, but I was very clear at that stage that I preferred our own consultant's 'wait and see' approach – he was always very conscious of making no real predictions and regularly admitted he did not know what was going on with Caroline. He told us that after Caroline was born we would have a better picture of how things were but admitted there was also a chance that we would never get answers about what had gone on. This was an honest viewpoint and left a hopeful outcome a continual possibility for us, although it did leave us perplexed about potentially never having answers. I felt this especially, as I do not like 'not knowing'.

It quickly became clear that I now faced the remainder of the pregnancy in hospital away from family, but this was balanced by the peace of mind I had in knowing the midwives would be monitoring Caroline closely and the knowledge that, however long the period seemed, our baby would soon be with us and we would be able to begin our lives (which were truly on hold) again.

9

NEARING THE END

By 11 August our consultant had returned from his holiday and was back at the helm. The baby's weight was now 2 lb 3 oz (990 g), which was a huge milestone for Colin and me. It was an increase of 130 grams since the previous scan, just one week before. We had not thought the baby would ever reach this weight, and we reminisced about the discussions that we had had when there was doubt that Caroline would ever make a viable weight of 500 or 600 g. She was almost double that now, and we still had at least a few weeks' growth left. My confidence was definitely growing at this stage. I genuinely felt if Caroline was going to call it a day she would have done it before now. She was battling to be born and seemed to be extremely strong and resilient given the length of time she had had to cope with critically limited resources.

I was now at thirty-five weeks' gestation. There was

no sign of me going into labour and this was positive on a number of levels. It was another great milestone, as the prematurity risks for the baby were now reducing at a great rate. Also, I had read that babies with skeletal dysplasias usually arrived early, at thirty-five weeks – I think due to the fluid levels often increasing because of the condition and bringing about premature labour. The Dopplers were unchanged and remained unchanged later that week, so nothing acute seemed imminent.

We could now occasionally observe Caroline making breathing movements, which was an encouraging sign that despite her size she was maturing in readiness for birth. Her gestational development (apart from growth) in the womb was matching a normal-sized baby almost exactly. She was breathing in amniotic fluid and we could see her little chest going in and out, practising for her birthday, which would not be too far off now. Nonetheless we still had the constant worry that things could change at any time. Life in the hospital was, also, starting to take its toll. I was getting increasingly tired as in a public ward other patients frequently came and went, and often needed treatment at night, which stopped me sleeping. Some nights I would only get two to three hours, followed by the same the next night, the only difference being the new group of women in early labour or on a drip to treat severe pregnancy sickness.

A typical day in the antenatal ward began at six o'clock

in the morning. I would be wakened to have my baby's heart rate checked and, simultaneously, I would be asked if the baby had been moving overnight. I frequently answered, 'I have no idea as I was asleep', which probably didn't go down very well. Even if I *had* woken the previous night and felt my baby move, I would need a minute to think back to it, but this question would be fired at me upon opening my eyes. Having experienced this for some time, I began to say, 'Yes' straight away, because I did think the question was a bit pointless; after all, the midwife was there 'listening in on baby', and I wondered if it made much difference what went on the previous night as long as the baby was happily breathing away there and now.

After a particularly bad few nights during which the ward was busy constantly, I asked Colin to get me earplugs to drown out some of the noise. The midwives were well used to my being a light sleeper; often they would not have to wake me to do their rounds, as I had been unable to get to sleep. The first night I used the earplugs I fell into a deep sleep. The combination of the lower volumes of noise and my total exhaustion from sleep deprivation in previous days had me comatose. The next morning a midwife who knew me well must have opened the curtains to check on Caroline. She probably called my name, but I did not respond. I don't know if she panicked, or simply upped her game in trying to wake me, but she shook me quite vigorously to get a response. I must have been in an action dream of some sort; I shot upright in the bed, roared, 'No' in a really loud voice, waking everyone in our ward, and rammed my rising head straight into her chest, sending her reeling backwards. When I woke fully, I saw her stricken face coming back into my cubicle as if the fear of God was in her; I had terrified her. I apologised and we both fell into fits of laughter. I warned everyone about the earplugs from then on and told them not to get too close if I was in a deep sleep.

Once the morning checks had been done at six o'clock, I could doze until seven o'clock, when the breakfast arrived. I found mealtimes were an important part of the day, because I was occupied for a while (and I love my food). After breakfast I would have a long shower to kill more time. At around eight or nine o'clock the consultant or a member of the team – which I always called 'the entourage' – would call in and check how things were. If there was anything to change or monitor, the midwives would be told. Most days there was little to report. At ten o'clock I would have the first trace of Caroline done. I hated this part of the day because Caroline tended to have a nap after breakfast and was never particularly active at this time. This was a problem because the midwives had to get reassuring data, with plenty of movement and good heart reactivity, to show the doctors. Some days I was left on this machine for up to two hours, when it was supposed to only take a few minutes. There was a rule that there had to be, I think, ten minutes of good data before the machine could be removed. But this could not be in two stages – it had to be continuous. If there was a break in the quality of the trace data, the ten minutes would have to be started again. Often Caroline would move and do all the right things for almost the required time, but it would not be enough, and I would be told, 'Just a few more minutes', which invariably stretched to longer. The midwives could get very busy: they could be caught up dealing with other patients and sometimes it seemed like they had forgotten I was on the trace; probably they were unable to get back to me because they were dealing with an emergency. If I rang the bell, having been on for a long time, they would sometimes have to get a doctor to check the trace before they would take it off, and of course the doctor would take forever to come. To be fair, this was all understandable in a busy antenatal ward, but when I was having traces twice a day I found it very tough sitting stationary for hours on end on my hospital bed.

One day my morning trace took two hours and fifteen minutes and my afternoon one two hours and ten minutes. Because there had been a heart-rate deceleration in the afternoon, I was put back on the trace machine that night for another two hours. In total, I spent six-and-a-half hours in one day having Caroline's CTGs done. I never complained because I knew all of this was happening for Caroline's good, and I knew how hard the staff at the hospital worked. They did an amazing job in good spirits under very busy and stressful working conditions, but it was very hard for me to stay upbeat, stuck on this machine much of the time.

One particular midwife was my saviour. She knew I was in for the long haul and knew Caroline's story well, as we chatted often. She would set me up on the trace, tell me to send for her immediately if the heart beat was lost, and return after twenty minutes, without fail. If the trace looked close to being okay, she would take it off straight away. If it wasn't very good, she would sit with me for a few more minutes and we would jig Caroline around to wake her until we got a few more minutes' decent reading. She made it her business to become familiar with Caroline's reactions on the trace and so could make an informed judgement quickly as to whether the situation was stable or changing. I used to smile and heave a sigh of relief when she was on duty, because I would invariably have a better day, be able to walk around and go into the corridor for a change of scene.

Lunch – a dinner and dessert – would be served at twelve o'clock. I looked forward to it and enjoyed it. I would then hope to have the machinery from the afternoon trace removed before visiting time, so that when friends and family called I wasn't stuck to the bed with my growing belly hanging out, strapped to a monitor. I resented it when the machinery was not removed in time, as visiting time was precious, giving me a chance to catch up with Colin and the boys, or spend time with family, who called very regularly, particularly my parents and siblings, who between them came every day. Visiting time could also be intensely stressful. I was always mindful that some of the women in the ward could be in early labour or very sick with Hyperemesis gravidarum – severe pregnancy sickness – and I would feel obliged to try to keep the children quiet. This could be tricky, depending on what mood they were in. They would get bored sitting quietly, and I felt guilty dragging them in there every day. They cheered me up a lot, however, bringing in art work and pictures they had drawn for me, which I stuck up all around the little bed space that I temporarily had to call home.

The Olympic Games were another saviour for me. I passed much time that summer watching the little portable television in the ward. If I wanted to watch it from my bed, I had to be quick in the morning; it could be seen from only two beds at a time, so an early start enabled me to angle it towards my side to get a better view.

The television was problematic at times, however. The first time was when I was watching the athletics at about five o'clock in the afternoon. Visiting time was over until later and I was enjoying the action. A man whose wife was in early labour was resting across the ward on her bed. He asked me to switch off the television because his wife was tired and, although I was a bit taken aback by the request,

I said I would for a while, so as not to be awkward. I sat bored for an hour or so and then decided to switch it back on. Within minutes the man reappeared from behind his wife's curtain and more or less told me this time to turn off the television. I took a split second to think before I replied. I told him I had been there three weeks and would possibly have to remain for another three; I said that while I had turned off the television for a while I would not be turning it off again. I explained that it was my only way of passing the time and reminded him that, within a day or so, he and his wife would be at home, where they could do what they liked with their own television, and I would be still here watching this one. He thought about arguing and then simply pulled the curtain back around the bed in a temper.

I thought he behaved a bit like a petulant child, but it could be argued that I did too. In my defence, I should say that if I was to stay sane I had to stick up for myself. I think if the woman herself had spoken to me, it might have been different, but I felt the man had no right to make demands in a female antenatal ward. In contrast, at other times, couples would come in for treatment, knowing they might be there for only a day or overnight, and they would treat the stay as some sort of holiday. They would be on a night out, short of the bottle of wine and the popcorn! On would go the television, at full volume, for the late-night movie, and I would spend the evening listening to their laughter and the film's soundtrack until a late hour. I felt like explaining that I was up every morning at six o'clock, and asking them to turn the television off at around eleven o'clock, but usually I didn't for fear of being a hypocrite. The midwives did look out for me, however, and they would often come in at final-check time and make comments such as, 'Will I switch off the lights now or in a few minutes?' Sometimes they would simply put the lights off to hint that people needed rest.

At the start of my time in the ward I was the ultimate Christian. If a woman was in labour I would help her and talk to her during contractions. I became good at sensing when women were progressing faster than they seemed to be. Often a woman would be given an internal examination and her cervix found to be three or four centimetres dilated – still a long way off the full ten-centimetre dilation that enables vaginal delivery – and would be told her delivery would be a long while yet. From my bed I could time the contractions and listen to the woman's reactions and could tell, sometimes very soon after the internal examination, that things had speeded up considerably. Having had children myself, I knew the signs of approaching delivery. On a few occasions I had to call the midwives on behalf of women who didn't want to call because they thought they were over-reacting to the pain; sure enough, they would be sent swiftly up to the labour ward in a wheelchair, having dilated to ten centimetres in the time that had passed.

I had particular sympathy for women who came in to be put on a drip because of serious pregnancy sickness. I had had bad experience of this myself and fully understood how awful it is. I would fetch extra sick buckets for them, or reassure them the sickness would all end before long, or call the nurses when they were very sick. After a while, however, my less Christian side emerged. If I struck up a connection with someone, I would look out for them, but I began to get weary of the retching and the moaning and groaning of the labouring women, especially at night. Their noise began to represent feelings of sickness and tiredness for me, and I am ashamed to say that near the end of my stay I used to think, 'Would you just shut up.' I suppose a sort of survival or self-preservation mechanism had to kick in so that I could look after myself and my own baby, first and foremost.

At four o'clock in the afternoon I would have my last meal of the evening – a salad or a fry. The lack of variety became a bit boring, but it was food, passed the time and kept me and Caroline going. Later came evening visiting time, during which I was usually very tired, as it ran until nine o'clock; having been awake since six o'clock in the morning – if I had managed to get to sleep at all – I was flagging by then. A friend who worked in the hospital used to visit regularly to get an update on Caroline and keep me company. I appreciated this as it passed the time and helped keep me sane. The only problem with visiting times was that they were so exhausting. Visitors would look to me to give them an update. Of course, they were worried about Caroline and wanted to know how things were. Whether I felt like talking about it or not, or indeed whether I wanted visitors or not, visiting times were a regular part of the day. For the most part, they were a welcome link with the outside world, but on occasion if I wasn't in good form, visiting times were a chore, but I could do or say nothing to curtail them, for fear of upsetting or insulting a visitor.

10

THE UPS AND DOWNS
OF HOSPITAL LIFE

While I was in the hospital, numerous patients came and went. All of them would hear about Caroline one way or another. Usually it was because of curiosity and something to talk about. They would all be shocked at her dimensions, because they compared her size with that of their own babies. Before long I could reel off the story without taking a breath and could anticipate the same disbelieving response every time. It was hard to build up much of a rapport with people because they would come and go so frequently, so I was thrilled midway through my stay when another woman came in with a baby with IUGR, a term I was so familiar with by now. She was in a bit of a state because the issue with her baby's growth had only recently been detected and she wasn't sure what was happening. It was her first baby too, which was unlucky for her. She was in the hospital for about a week as a private patient. Once we had struck up an impromptu friendship, however, she dismissed the idea of pushing for a private room and was content to have a laugh and a chat in the ward. She and I discovered we had mutual friends in 'the outside world' (the term I had increasingly come to use in referring to life beyond the ward). She introduced me to brain training on her Nintendo and I chatted with her about motherhood.

We got on well, I think, because we could each appreciate what the other was going through. We had a great laugh some days as she had a very dry sense of humour. Her baby was born at 4 lb 14 oz (2.21 kg) at about thirty-five weeks, and thrived, which was brilliant. Even after she had been discharged from the hospital, she would sometimes pop up to say hello to me when she was returning to see her baby in the neonatal unit. We were as giddy as two teenagers on occasion. Once she told me a story about a father in the unit who was accusing other mothers and the midwives of stealing his wife's breast milk. My friend said he was very odd and his wife never spoke, but he thought he was running the show down in the neonatal unit. I realised immediately I had met this couple before, only weeks earlier, in my ward. It emerged over time that the milk was being moved to a reserve fridge, of which he wasn't aware, because so many mothers were expressing for their babies at the time.

In the meantime, however, our imaginations went berserk

and we whiled away many an hour concocting stories of who the milk thief could be. We played out scenarios akin to those of Inspector Clouseau depicting who the culprit might be and making up reports such as: 'A top hospital obstetrician and gynaecologist has been charged with stealing lactating mothers' breast milk. The discovery was made after a distinctive milk moustache was observed on the accused gynaecologist's face at morning rounds yesterday.' The imagery and sheer juvenile nature of this carry-on kept me going, and for a few days any consultant who walked in sent us into fits of laughter again as we imagined scanning him for that giveaway milk moustache. I'd say some people thought we were soft in the head, and possibly very rude too, but they will get over it. It did us good and made us smile when life was dull. We still send the odd text and keep in touch. It was a pleasure to make a connection with someone when I was in hospital for such a long time.

When visiting hours were over each day, there would be a cup of tea and a biscuit and then a wait for the change of staff so the evening rounds could be done and I could go to sleep. Sometimes these rounds would happen quite late, so I would ask to have the blood-pressure and baby checks done a little earlier. Often in the middle of the night people would be admitted to the ward, which made things difficult for me. Some midwives would march in, put on all the lights and talk; it seemed to me as if it were the middle of the day rather than three o'clock in the morning. They would loudly show the newly admitted person the bathroom – squeaky door and all – do all their observations, chat and laugh with each other while they were working, and leave up to an hour later. I know this must sound so whiney now, but when this happened three or four times a week, sometimes more than once a night, it soon became highly irritating. I knew I would be sick with tiredness all the next day, as catching up on rest during the day was impossible. The routine of the hospital between medical observations, doctors' rounds, cleaning crews' activities, mealtimes and visiting times meant that if I didn't sleep at night, I didn't sleep at all. I wasn't one of those enviable women who could nod off at the drop of a hat. My discovery of the earplugs, although hazardous to midwives' health, hugely benefited me in at least dulling the noise.

Sometimes, late into the evening, our consultant would be on duty and would call to speak to a new admission he was treating in the private system. This patient might be in a ward until a private room became available. Not once did the consultant call to speak to a private patient without popping his head around my curtain just to say hello and ask how things were with Caroline and me. I thought this was a kind gesture; he fully espoused a sense of equality among his patients, regardless of whether they were private or public. We were people first and patients second, and he seemed to disregard any public–private distinction.

The counsellor came occasionally, too, to see how things were. I benefited from her approach. For example on one occasion, when I had been awake all night because the ward was busy and the previous night had not been much better, I was extremely weary and very close to bailing out and going home. A doctor who came into my ward to do a check found me in tears and asked me what was wrong. I felt like saying, 'How long have you got and where would you like me to start?' However, I just replied that I was exhausted from lack of sleep. The doctor looked at me as if to say, 'You wouldn't be in tears just because you are tired', explaining to me in what seemed to me like a pull-yourself-together way that stress wouldn't be doing my baby any good. At this point I almost laughed out loud; Caroline had not had one single day since fourteen weeks when I had not been pumping corticosteroid hormones into her due to the stress I had been experiencing. It was an irony that this stress was directly caused by hospital life; it was manifesting in me because of the circumstances I had to endure. I wanted to ask this doctor to swap places with me for forty-eight hours and see how they felt. The most frustrating thing of all was that they didn't seem to believe I could be so distressed due to lack of sleep. I later found it written in my notes, which I read daily to pass the time, that I should be watched for depression. I have no prejudices about depressed people or depression, but I knew I did not have depression and it made me angry that this person hadn't listened and had exhibited no understanding or sympathy for my situation.

Shortly after the doctor had left, the counsellor arrived, clearly summoned to check me out. She listened sympathetically and thought the depression idea was an over-reaction. She spoke to the ward manager and it was arranged that, if possible, my ward would be left until last to be filled that evening – and, because it was due to be quiet, there was a good chance no one would be coming in that night. I got one solid night of sleep from then on every few days or so, and I managed on that. The difference between the doctor's and the counsellor's approach to the problem was astounding to me; one seemed to view me purely from a medical perspective, while the other looked at the bigger picture, listened to what I was saying and did something to help. I was grateful to the counsellor for her approach. Most midwives, too, were supportive and professional and made life easier during my hospital stay; they would chat when they had time and listen to my own theories about what might have happened with Caroline.

I think if someone is in hospital for a long stay, they should be given some time in a private room regardless of whether they are private or public patients. I found it exhausting to have to make acquaintances over and over again, as new patients were admitted, only to see them leave within a day or two. The lack of privacy was horrendous:

if I was having a bad day there was nowhere to hide and be alone. As Colin pointed out, sleep deprivation is a form of torture and a recognised interrogation method in many countries, and now I can really appreciate why. I was often close to ringing a taxi and walking out. I became so desperate at times that I even found myself thinking that I did not care what happened to the baby; I just wanted privacy, space and sleep.

The toughest challenge was having to explain repeatedly the reason I was in hospital, as the only conversation other patients could strike up began: 'What are you in for?' I resented having to tell everyone about Caroline and explain the issues regarding her size. I got sick of the shocked reaction people showed when they heard how small she was. Early on, too, going over the whole thing with the midwives until all shifts knew the story with Caroline exhausted me. Often I felt like saying, 'Just read the notes', but I did not want to fall out with people when I knew I would be there for a while. In fairness, the staff were brilliant, but I resented having to be in hospital, missed my family and many times wondered if I would lose my mind with nothing to do all day but wait and worry and wonder. Of course, there was a lot of doing-the-deal-with-God: promises of praying regularly, going to Mass every Sunday, literally a you-name-it-and-I-will-do-it approach to bargaining in return for a healthy baby. Scary and weird stuff often went through my head in those lonely days. I remember imagining a person asking me, 'Would you lose a finger to have Caroline born okay?' or 'What about a hand or kidney?' In hindsight, these were clearly manifestations of the intense stress I was under and perhaps ways of punishing myself for not being able to grow a baby properly or for having another baby at thirty-seven years of age, when I was lucky enough to have three already. I can safely say, however, that at that time I would have done virtually anything to see Caroline healthy and safely delivered.

But one group of women had things worse than me – much worse. These were the women with placenta praevia – a condition in which the placenta develops in a very low position in the uterus, sometimes blocking the birth canal. It can be serious because, as the baby gets bigger and heavier, this can put pressure on the placenta – which is essentially the baby's lifeline – and bleeding can start. As soon as a woman with placenta praevia is diagnosed – usually at the first scan, or a little later – she is warned to watch for bleeding and get herself admitted to hospital if it starts. Once these women are in hospital, they seem to stay for a long period. If the bleed is very small and stops quickly, they seem to have some chance of going home speedily, but any significant bleeding means they are kept in for observation. When I was in the hospital there was one woman who had had a bleed at eighteen weeks and she spent the remainder of her pregnancy in the hospital.

Sometimes, as the uterus enlarges and grows up and out, it pulls the placenta up with it out of its very low position. If this happens to a woman, she can usually leave the hospital, but if not, she may very well have to stay for months on end. A good number of women came in with bleeding while I was there and the medical staff could not stop it despite their best efforts. Inevitably labour would begin, and the babies were usually too small to survive. These women must have felt as though they were carrying a potential time bomb that could go off without notice. I know from talking to them that they experienced similar stress to me, not in the sense that there was anything wrong with their babies but through the worry of what might happen unexpectedly on any day.

After I had been in the hospital for about two or three weeks, and Caroline had settled down and was having no further decelerations on her traces, it was decided I might be allowed out for an hour once or twice a week. This was funny, really, as the procedure for obtaining permission was similar to that I imagine is needed for getting a temporary home visit from prison. It had to be in my notes and was checked and double-checked. I was warned not to walk for long, but instead just to go over to a local hotel for a coffee and sit down. I enjoyed these times, as I could go with the children somewhere where I did not have to worry so much about their behaviour. We had a pleasant few hours over my last few weeks in the hospital chatting, away from the stress of ward life. The hardest part was returning, however; I had to get back into my pyjamas and onto the bed, staring at the four walls, with strangers for company. I used to feel awful going back, so much so that in the last week I chose not to go out, both for Caroline's sake – in case something happened away from the hospital – and because I knew I didn't have long to go. Another woman who was in the hospital for a while used to go 'AWOL', as I called it. She would disappear for hours – I think she went home. She was told in no uncertain terms that she would quickly lose the privilege of being allowed out of hospital if she didn't respect it, which was fair enough, I suppose. Being in hospital was a little prison-like in some respects, endured all for the safety of the babies we were carrying.

11

PREPARING TO DELIVER

At thirty-six weeks Caroline's weight took an impressive leap from 990 g to 1.161 kg (2 lb 8 oz). This made the wait in hospital worthwhile. Caroline was still making breathing movements visible on the scans, which was proof that she was continuously maturing despite still being very small. The time had come to discuss a definite delivery plan. The consultant felt that the balance of risk now favoured definite delivery at thirty-seven weeks, only one week later. Prematurity was negligible given the gestational age we had unexpectedly reached. The weight was relatively good, considering where Caroline had come from. I was booked in to be induced the following Tuesday. With another week's growth to go, we could only feel confident that I would deliver a live baby.

Caroline's health remained to be seen, of course, but we really had come a long way. I was thrilled, but apprehensive, that I could attempt to deliver naturally and possibly avoid a major operation. I was made aware, however, that it was by no means guaranteed that the baby would tolerate the induction. This week was also special as we went to visit the neonatal unit, which would be Caroline's home for a good many weeks after her delivery. It required a code to get in and was highly secure – we had to give our identity before being let in. We travelled down a corridor and entered the first section of the unit, to the left – the intensive-care section for very ill babies. The lights were dim and everyone was speaking in hushed tones. Many babies in this section are extremely premature and should still be in the womb for months. They do not tolerate loud noises very well and do better if the environment is as stress free as possible. There were a good number of babies in large incubators with quilt-like covers to maintain a dark, quiet place for them to sleep and grow. These babies wore only a nappy and nearly all were being fed by tube. Each incubator had monitors checking the oxygen saturation, heart rate and breathing of the baby inside. These were all calibrated to safe levels; if any baby moved outside these parameters an alarm would go off and the staff would investigate the problem. Each midwife was assigned a number of babies, although if a baby was very ill it would have one-to-one care around the clock.

I was desperate to see a baby of a similar size to Caroline, but the closest we could get was a baby boy who weighed 3 lb 8 oz (1.59 kg). Even at that weight, he was tiny; this really brought it home to us how small Caroline would be. Some of the babies were being fully ventilated; others were on CPAP – a system that assists weak babies who are breathing on their own, but missing occasional breaths, by filling in the gaps until the babies are strong enough to breathe completely on their own. We wondered how Caroline's breathing would be, dreading the tubes and medical devices she would have to tolerate, but we knew this care would be essential to her continued survival.

The next room in the neonatal unit was the high-dependency room, for babies who were out of intensive care. Here the babies were bigger and some were out of the incubators and in little cots. This room was smaller, with a few screened-off little rooms for babies who were infectious or needed isolation for some reason. The final room was the special-care room – the final stopping point for babies in the unit before they went home. It contained babies who were closer to normal birth weights but who had feeding difficulties or other issues in the early stages of their lives. Many would pay only a short visit here before going back to their mothers in the wards. All these babies were dressed and in cots. None had feeding tubes or patterned quilt-like covers surrounding the incubators to block out the light. There were still monitors, but these was far smaller and less sophisticated, and this made the room quieter. The few parents who were in the unit feeding babies or visiting differed starkly from room to room. There was a tension in the intensive-care section, which had less chit-chat or laughter. The high-dependency room seemed a little more relaxed. In the special-care room there was lots of interaction with the babies and between the parents. I knew where I wanted to be with Caroline and, as I left, I thought, 'We are going to get you in here, Caroline, as soon as we can, and then out and home.' Everyone we met knew about Caroline and had been briefed on her condition and why she was coming. She really was becoming quite the little celebrity.

On 22 August, approaching a miraculous thirty-seven weeks – a figure that officially represented full term for a baby's development – the consultant and I met to check whether a natural delivery might be feasible. We debated once more leaving Caroline in the womb for another week to facilitate her putting on a few more ounces, against risking losing her altogether if her condition was to worsen unexpectedly. This gestational age was never expected to be reached but, because Caroline was making some growth and did not appear to be worsening in terms of the Doppler readings as each week went by, we had continually aimed for week after week. However, at this stage we decided the benefits of leaving Caroline in the uterus were outweighed by the potential risk of something bad happening, as my already imperfect placenta would age and become even less efficient as I approached the end of pregnancy.

The days preceding the delivery were exciting but also very tense in case something unexpected happened just as we were almost there and also because we were finally going to find out how Caroline would cope on her own, outside me.

Caroline had made it to the 1-kg mark (approximately 2 lb 8 oz), far beyond the 500 g or 600 g that we had been hoping to make only a few weeks before. Table 1 shows Caroline's weight at selected weeks of her gestation.

Table 1: Caroline's weight at selected weeks of gestation

Gestation in actual weeks	Weight in grams	Weight in pounds and ounces
14 weeks	Unknown	Unknown
20 weeks	125 g	4 oz
22 weeks	174 g	6 oz
24 weeks	249 g	9 oz
26 weeks	297 g	10 oz
27 weeks	341 g	12 oz
28 weeks	472 g	1 lb 1 oz
29 weeks	536 g	1 lb 3 oz
30 weeks	579 g	1 lb 4 oz
31 weeks	704 g	1 lb 9 oz
32 weeks	784 g	1 lb 12 oz
33 weeks	825 g	1 lb 13 oz
34 weeks	860 g	1 lb 15 oz
35 weeks	990 g	2 lb 3 oz
36 weeks	1,161 g	2 lb 8 oz

She was still shockingly small for a full-term baby, and her weight equated to that of a foetus only twenty-seven or twenty-eight weeks old. It was impossible to imagine properly how small Caroline was going to be, despite the visit to the neonatal unit.

For her birth, an operating theatre was booked, in case complications made a Caesarean section necessary, given Caroline's size, but to my surprise our consultant was willing to give a natural vaginal delivery an attempt. I was highly relieved at this, as I had been hoping not to go through another section and the painful recovery that follows one. I was more than aware that Caroline would be staying in the neonatal unit for some time to grow, and I wanted to be well enough to drive to and from the hospital from home to see her, which would be impossible after an operation. I think most other doctors and midwives thought this plan was unlikely and possibly unwise, as I suppose the more controlled delivery, given Caroline's unknown health, would have been a section. But our consultant and ourselves had never followed the crowd and did things based on Caroline, not just on the medical textbooks, which may have called for a far earlier delivery due to the severity of her intrauterine growth restriction. There were a few raised eyebrows and surprised reactions when staff on the antenatal ward heard the plan, but our consultant, Colin and I were willing to give a vaginal birth a try; we knew it would be monitored closely and that I would be sectioned immediately if anything even looked like going wrong. We did not intend to take any chances with a baby who had come this far, despite poor odds.

Nonetheless I knew many small babies – some smaller than Caroline – had been safely delivered naturally. That evening I got my diary out and spent literally hours poring over my tables (see Table 1) and graphs of Caroline's development. I read the specialists' notes and predictions and my diary extracts to relive the journey thus far. I could not believe that we were almost at the end of the pregnancy and that there was a chance Caroline would survive. I knew we still did not have a clear idea of how she would be, but I was hopeful again and my gut – which had told me all those months ago that Caroline was inside me – strongly indicated to me now that things would be okay. I felt a huge sense of peace and settled down to try to sleep.

At this final meeting on 22 August, just four days short of the magic thirty-seven-week mark for Caroline, our consultant did an internal examination to assess how ripe my cervix was – was it showing any signs of readiness for delivery given that we were still a few weeks early? As he said, if it was like 'Fort Knox', there might be difficulty in getting it ready for a vaginal delivery. He warned me if it was unripe he would manipulate it a bit to encourage it to start dilating a little. The examination revealed that the cervix was fairly tightly closed, but after an uncomfortable minute or so of manipulation, we hoped that, over the next twenty-four hours, it would react to the stimulation. At the same time as doing the internal examination, the consultant also pushed Caroline's head down manually towards the cervix to get it to engage and so assist with downward pressure on the cervix to make it open. All we could do now was wait and see if any developments would occur overnight.

That evening, to my disappointment, when a midwife came to listen to Caroline's heart, she mentioned that Caroline was in a breech position – she had her feet, not her head, towards the cervix. Perhaps Caroline intended to kick her way out (it wouldn't have surprised me in the least), but really it meant a vaginal delivery was impossible unless she changed position again. It was typical of Caroline to insist on controlling things right to the last. She was letting us know this was all about her and of course, being so small, she, unlike other thirty-seven-week foetuses, had ample space to move even at this stage.

I went to sleep that night almost resigned to the fact I would be operated on within forty-eight hours. The next morning, having barely slept, as was usually the case in a busy ward, I awoke to thoughts that this day would be my last day ever as a pregnant woman. It was a very pleasant thought actually, as this pregnancy had been so tough that there was no way I would risk another one. All I wanted to do was see Caroline and start my life again. Of course, I knew life would not be easy for a while, or possibly ever again, but this was still better than the tension of not knowing answers to the questions I kept asking myself about how Caroline would be after birth.

The family were all coming in to the hospital that afternoon for the final of many scans throughout the pregnancy. I could not help but think back to the day we had first met the consultant, when he had mentioned quite casually that the baby was measuring a little behind expectations in terms of growth. He had not been worried, as a miscalculation of dates would easily explain this, but I had known something was wrong. I had heard of a mother's intuition and had thought it was rubbish, like most abstract concepts. I remembered the times I had broken down in the scan room as week after week Caroline had put on only an ounce or two, which was disastrous. I thought about the constant questions I had put to the consultant and the amateur potential diagnoses I had come up with. He had put up with a huge amount of hassle and, of course, I was just one of many patients he was seeing, some possibly with worse problems. Even though I could sometimes read stress on his face, he never ever got cross or insensitive, and anything we asked of him he tried his best to deliver (again, pardon the pun). He was superbly efficient, professional and, most importantly, human. We will never be able to thank him enough.

Before the scan the consultant wanted to do a final internal examination to see if my cervix had improved. He had been told about the breech position and felt it was unlikely Caroline would turn back in time, but said he would check how things were anyway. My cervix had dilated quite well and was much more ready for birth, which was good news. In addition, the consultant mentioned, a little unsurely, that he thought Caroline had turned head downwards again. I could not believe it. It appeared everything was back on track for a natural delivery, when only hours before this had been highly unlikely. The scan was to be the final decider on whether an induction of labour would be attempted the following morning. All of us piled into the scan room and the consultant very kindly explained everything on the screen to the children. He showed them Caroline's face, tiny hands, feet and backbone. They were amazed as he referred to their new sister and presented them all with a little scan picture to keep for themselves. He took as much time answering their questions and chatting naturally with them as scanning. I had an enormous lump in my throat, as I am sure Colin did, as it was clear that if the delivery and hours after birth didn't go well, these would be the last live memories any of us would have of Caroline. We were very grateful for the consultant's kindness at this scan, but were not surprised at it, as we had experienced many other examples of such kindness throughout the long pregnancy. It was a poignant and memorable time for us all, filled with apprehension but at the same time merged with huge hope.

The scan revealed that Caroline was indeed in a cephalic – or head-down – position. Not only that, she was well engaged in the pelvis and ready to be born naturally. I often imagine Caroline as a bit of a prankster at that time, stirring things up every now and then as if we didn't have enough excitement already! I said goodbye to Colin and the children and knew the next time I saw Colin would be the next day when my labour was started. Of course I half expected to be ringing him an hour later to tell him Caroline had somersaulted again, but that didn't happen. Although Colin and I talked for hours on the phone that evening once the children had gone to bed, Caroline behaved herself and stayed put for the night.

12

CAROLINE'S BIRTHDAY

The weirdest thing that happened the night before Caroline's birthday was that I actually got some sleep. I don't know how or why, but I was grateful to wake up feeling relatively fresh and ready to deliver my long-awaited daughter. Things were all falling into place, or so I thought. At 7.30 a.m., an hour or so later than planned, a registrar arrived to insert two pessaries designed to gradually soften and dilate my cervix further and get labour started. I was also attached to a heart trace machine for Caroline to be monitored and to see how she was tolerating the induction. I was pleased that within half an hour I was experiencing mild contractions, indicating that the induction was working as planned.

No sooner had I lain back to relax while I could in view of the long day ahead, than I felt a contraction start and then heard a sound I had heard on Caroline's previous traces only twice before, but which was familiar to me, having spent five weeks in an antenatal ward with labouring women. It was the characteristic heartbeat of my baby slowing down from its rhythmic speedy beat to a slow, threatening one. It was the most frightening sound, as the heartbeat slowed quickly and I was anticipating that it would stop. It usually climbs up slowly again, but leaves the listener terrified. I pressed the buzzer to call for help. As I did so, it happened again. Caroline's heart did a massive deceleration, and now I was panicking. Something was very wrong. I thought for a split second that after everything Caroline was going to die.

The midwife arrived and I told her what had happened. She looked at the trace, which was now printing the terrible evidence. The decelerations I had heard appeared equally massive on paper. The midwife acted in a very matter-of-fact way when she said she was going to get a registrar, but I was well versed in the subtle body language I had observed for so long and knew she was worried. Within minutes a registrar, whom we had met before and who knew Caroline's case well, came in and had a look at the trace. He said he couldn't tell what was wrong without doing an internal examination, but he warned me that in order to get the full picture he would have to get his fingers inside the still fairly closed cervix and that it would be extremely painful. He got a nurse to hold my hand and asked me not to move but to squeeze her hand if I needed to. It was a moment of agony, and I involuntarily let out a roar. I remember instinctively pushing his hand away, even though I knew it had to be done. I thought I would be sick but before that happened it was over and he sat on the bed. He explained that the internal examination, although painful, had given him extremely valuable information. He was able to feel Caroline's head above the cervix but also the cord across the top of it. What was happening was that every time I had a contraction, Caroline's head was pushing as it should do on my cervix to dilate it, but the cord had slipped under her head at some stage due to her small size, and every time she pushed down she cut off her own oxygen supply by compressing the cord.

It was clearly explained that if I proceeded with a natural delivery I would be taking a huge risk. I was advised to have an emergency Caesarean section there and then. The registrar would operate and I would have Caroline out within ten minutes. Although I was disappointed, there was no real decision to make. I could not risk Caroline's health or life because I was scared of an operation. I said I was ready to go ahead with the section but that I would have to be put under general anaesthetic. No one commented at this point about the anaesthetic but proceeded to get me gowned up, dry shaved down below for reasons of sterility during the operation and promptly plopped into a wheelchair to be wheeled down to the operating theatre. I had literally thirty seconds to ring Colin to tell him to get to the hospital as fast as he could as there was a complication and I was having a Caesarean section. As is typical of Colin, he began asking questions and mentioned that my parents had not yet arrived from their house to mind the other children, as though I could do anything about that! I reminded him quite forcefully that Caroline was being delivered in a few minutes by Caesarean section and that I needed him there, so he would need to sort out the problems somehow. I think a few of the midwives felt I was a bit unfair on him and were possibly surprised at me, as I had been fairly well behaved while in the hospital, but, really, what else could I say?

As I was wheeled down to the operating theatre, I was telling anyone who would listen that I wanted to be put out for the operation. This preference stemmed from having been awake for my first son David's birth by Caesarean section; to this day I remember the fear of that delivery, which I felt I was too much a part of, and I did not want to experience that again – I had had nightmares afterwards for months. I saw the operating theatre doors being held open by a midwife and took a deep breath as I was wheeled in. The idea of going willingly and fully awake into a fully equipped operating theatre is still, to my mind, bizarre beyond belief. As I entered I looked knowingly around as I had been in this very room before, with its many people – far more than I would have expected – dutifully attending to their roles before an operation. I could see the scalpels, swabs and other glistening pieces of equipment being laid out for the second time, and it was no better for my nerves this time, despite my having come through the experience before. Out of the corner of my eye I saw an incubator and silently hoped Caroline would be born well. Anaesthetists, doctors, neonatal nurses, a paediatrician and the surgeon were there; the place was packed, ready for a baby who had by now become famous among the hospital population. Everyone I had spoken to for the final week in hospital had been briefed on the impending birth of the smallest full-term baby the hospital or any of its obstetricians had ever seen.

I was wheeled over to a tiny narrow table on wheels, on which I would be operated on. The anaesthetist introduced himself and explained that a spinal block would be inserted into my back to numb me for the procedure. I felt like shouting, 'Hasn't anyone been listening to me?' but simply repeated that I was terrified of being awake again for a Caesarean. This clearly was not forceful enough, as I was told I would be fine and that as soon as Caroline was out they would sedate me to calm me down. For a split second I prepared literally to run out of the doors as no one had a hold of me, but I couldn't move. I gave up the fight and simply mumbled 'Okay' as I was manoeuvred onto the table and bent double to have the local anaesthetic administered.

At this point I felt totally and utterly demoralised. I felt like a piece of old luggage that simply served to carry this baby around for nine months. It seemed everything – from needing sleep, sympathy and peace, to my choice of whether I would be cut open and rummaged in awake or asleep – was out of my control. Everyone else was deciding what would happen, I felt, probably irrationally, to suit themselves. Yes, of course, it is probably safer to use a spinal block, as the baby receives none of the general anaesthetic drug, but realistically the baby is out within ten minutes or less, so how much would really pass through to her in this time?

I wanted to be asleep for a few reasons. They were my bad experience of being awake at David's Caesarean birth and the question of what would happen if there was a massive emergency once Caroline was out and she did not breathe or had died during the process. This would leave me with those panicked moments as my last memories of her failed fight for survival. There I would be, strapped to a table being stitched up, while all the time I would be hearing and seeing my baby's last breaths. I wanted to miss that potential disaster and remember Caroline in the womb happily jigging about the previous evening; if I woke to bad news I would imagine my own scenario, which would be a calm and peaceful end.

This was not to be, however, and as I felt the sharp prick of the local anaesthetic, followed by the pressured push of the delivery canula for the spinal drugs, I clenched my fists together and told myself I had to get through this ordeal only once more, ever. At this stage I was unaware of how close Colin would come to missing the birth; since my parents had not arrived when I rang, thinking it would be a long, slow, normal vaginal delivery, he was frantically ringing neighbours' doorbells to see if someone could hold the fort with the other children until my parents arrived. It would have been such a shame if Colin had not been present, as he had travelled the same journey as me every step of the way and had been present at the births of all our children.

It took little time for the spinal block to take effect, and I was asked if I could feel any pain as they prodded my legs and abdomen with a sharp needle. I could feel no pain, but could sense the pressure, which was normal. Lying back on the bed, I felt sick and started to panic, as I knew I would. A large green piece of fabric was placed directly in front of my face to shield the view if I were to sit up. I remembered this from the previous time and I began to feel very claustrophobic. Colin came in as I was trying to push it out of the way but the anaesthetist had a firm grip of my hand and was soothingly telling me to calm down. I began to hyperventilate with the fear and had an oxygen mask promptly fixed to my mouth as I think my blood pressure was altering. This did not help the claustrophobia one bit. Soon I became aware of a sensation that felt as though someone was drawing a line with felt pen low down on my abdomen. Again I remembered feeling this before and the vision of me being cut open flooded my head. I shouted to them that I could feel it – not pain but sensation – and they stopped for a second to try to calm me before insisting that I was mistaken. Seconds later the rummaging began. This would be difficult for anyone who has not experienced it to imagine: I could clearly feel the surgeon's hands inside my abdomen and it was quite uncomfortable. I heard the suction tubes removing the amniotic fluid and then the tugging and pulling began. I heard the surgeon mention that Caroline was breech and I thought, 'There you are again dancing around right to the end.' It seemed like forever before the pressure on my chest, which felt at times like a heavy weight, ended and the tugging stopped. Caroline was born; it was 9.15 a.m. on 26 August 2008.

I did not get to see Caroline immediately as I had with David eight years before, as she was not breathing immediately and was taken to be ventilated. At this stage I felt very calm and as though I was looking on all the frantic activity through someone else's eyes. It was then that one of the nurses asked me if I was feeling calmer and it dawned on me that the promise of sedation had been fulfilled. Caroline had her Apgar scores taken – these scores assess the baby's responses and pallor and are indicators of the initial health of the baby. Caroline's score was five at one minute old but nine at five minutes old, which was excellent. It was at this time that I heard Caroline cry for the very first time and I joined her. She had the weakest, highest-pitched little squeak of a cry I had ever heard. Her tiny lungs did not possess the power to make a lusty-baby cry, but still it was like magic, hearing her voice. Sadly, Caroline was then quickly whisked away to the neonatal unit, with Colin catching a glance as she left. Although I was elated she had been born and was alive, I was devastated not to have seen her. It felt again as though I did not matter: I was just the baby's mother, the vessel in which she grew so poorly. I completely understood that she needed to be taken care of, but I felt cheated that all these medical people were the first to see my precious daughter and I would have to wait hours and hours before I could set eyes on her. We were given a picture at some stage later that day, but it was a Polaroid one in which it was quite difficult to see Caroline's face.

Caroline weighed in at 2 lb 9 oz or 1.18 kg at exactly thirty-seven weeks' gestation. Our daughter had arrived, and she was doing well according to reports filtering from the neonatal unit. The placenta – which was thought to have been at least partly responsible for Caroline's poor growth – was delivered and I heard the surgeon mention that it too was unhealthily small. Having been stitched up, I was wheeled back to my familiar spot in the antenatal ward to begin my five-day recovery period before going home. I was grateful to be allowed back to an antenatal ward, as spending time in a postnatal ward, with all the other women feeding, admiring and cuddling their babies, would have been tough.

Colin spent a while ringing everyone to tell them the news while I dozed in a blissful haze of sedation and strong painkillers. Whether it was the relief that Caroline was at last born and the dreadful pregnancy was over, or the drugs, I can safely say I have never felt so chilled out in my life. I was without a care in the world for a few hours until concern and the need to see Caroline for myself intensified again. I plagued Colin for details of how Caroline looked from the glance he had had and asked him specifically if she looked normal. Of course a starved and emaciated baby is never going to look like a normal chubby one, but what I meant was: were her features normal-looking? Everyone told me she looked normal for her size, which did warn me she would be much different from her siblings at birth.

Colin went down to the neonatal unit about an hour after the birth to see her. When he returned he was full of emotion. He told me Caroline was beautiful and not quite as small-looking as he had expected. He had only been able to look at her through the incubator glass in her tiny nappy, tubes everywhere, with her face masked by her ventilator, but already he was totally smitten. I knew from that moment on Caroline would be a daddy's girl and that she would have him wrapped tightly around her little finger before long. I was not wrong!

At about four o'clock the nurses were probably sick of me asking to go to the unit to see Caroline and gave in.

First, however, they said I would need to stand and go to the bathroom to change pads and wash. I had memories of this also from the last time and knew it would be tough. I do not know of any other operation where a patient is forced to walk five or six hours after major surgery. Apparently it helps recovery considerably but it is quite painful. The nurses helped me sit up first and gently swung my legs over the side of the bed. Then I was told to take a deep breath and, with two nurses helping me, I was pulled to a standing position. I felt dizzy and extremely nauseous and started to gag; they suggested I get back into bed and try later when I had rested more. I knew this would mean I would not be allowed to see Caroline, so I insisted I was okay and took a step. It felt as if my insides were about to fall out and, as if on cue, a massive blood clot made its exit onto the floor, over my new blue stripy slippers. I weakened more at the sight of this than at anything else, but as it was being cleaned away I took another step. Each step became easier and, dragging my drip along beside me, I made the few paces to the bathroom.

I had proven I was well enough to get out of bed; a wheelchair was found and I sat in it to go to see Caroline. I couldn't contain my excitement: at last I was going to see this baby I had dreamed of night after night. I felt every bump as Colin wheeled me into the lift to go down the single floor to the neonatal unit. We pressed the buzzer at the neonatal unit's entrance and, after what seemed like forever, a nurse let us in. We travelled down the corridor and turned left into the intensive-care section. In the muted light, the only sounds were the beeps of the machinery and the voices of the staff doing their work. Colin wheeled me over to an incubator opposite the door; there Caroline was, sound asleep with a gorgeous little woolly hat on her head, and nothing else on but her nappy. By now she was off the ventilator and was breathing on her own, with a CPAP machine covering the odd breath she might not automatically take by herself. She was so thin and frail-looking, with her nasal tube appearing far too big for her little face. Facially, she looked quite battered. She had marks, some of which were birthmarks which faded within days, under her nose and on her forehead. Although a healthy pink, her skin looked sore. Her hairline had not developed fully, which made her look like a balding old man with a receding hairline and she had irregular patches around her skull. Her nose looked slightly upturned and too big for her face, and her cheeks were hauntingly hollow and devoid of any fat whatsoever. Her eyes were missing eyelashes; her eyebrows were absent too. Her lips looked a little swollen but her ears were beautiful. I was quite shocked when I saw her, because she was not pretty yet, but I loved her with all my heart and I knew, with the fight she had in her, she would soon fill out and develop her facial features. I was fascinated watching her heavy breathing and regular twitches and shudders, with the odd look around with just one eye open.

As I sat watching her I began to feel woozy. It was understandably very warm in the unit and I was exhausted from the physical and emotional challenges of the day. My parting words to Caroline that first afternoon were not charged with love but were frantic calls for a sick bowl. It was handed to me and I was wheeled at speed towards the corridor to avoid introducing infection into the unit, with its sick babies. I just made the corridor before I was violently sick, to be taken back to the ward shaking and green. I wasn't even able to say goodbye to Caroline, but I knew now that I was on my feet, I would be able to visit her whenever I wanted and I looked forward to that.

Once I was back in bed, Colin needed to get back home to the other children so we said our goodbyes. It was strange for both of us, as for our other three pregnancies Colin had not left me alone – we had left together, with our new baby. Nevertheless, we felt very lucky to have Caroline with us and I knew, even though she had a long way to go, that she would pull through and start to grow. I was given an injection to stop the vomiting, as it was inclined to linger into the evening, and I closed my eyes to end one of the best days of my life. Along with the birth of our other children and our wedding day, this was a special day. I felt content, complete and just happy, a feeling I had missed for a whole seven months since that first fateful scan. I took time to contemplate how lucky we were. Two babies had died just days before as they had been premature and too small to survive. My heart went out to their parents. I thought I could imagine how it must have felt, as I had prepared for a similar fate at moments along our journey, but Caroline thankfully had made it through the birth, although we were told the next forty-eight hours would be crucial.

That evening I stopped to reflect also on how lucky I was to have Colin. He had been so strong and positive throughout the pregnancy. He had constantly repeated to me that Caroline would make it. He had believed it and felt it – and who knows the power of that positivity? He had sat with me through the lowest moments and listened to my fears and worries. Most of all he had endured five whole weeks on his own, with no help, looking after our other children through the summer – feeding, dressing and washing them, and keeping them happy by playing with them. He had brought them into the hospital – a thirty-mile round trip – every day and occasionally twice a day so I could spend time with them. They, and he, had kept me going through the long and arduous hospital stay. For that I will be eternally grateful. He is, and remains, my soulmate, the only person I can rely on for anything in life I need and the person who loves me for who I am. I love him dearly and could not have made it to Caroline's birthday sanely if it had not been for him. As I drifted off to sleep I know I had a smile on my face. Caroline had been born and was breathing on her own, against all the odds.

13

GOING HOME WITHOUT
MY BABY

The morning after Caroline's birthday I woke up sore and tired, but nonetheless I was a woman on a mission. Before breakfast, I slowly made my way down to see Caroline. Getting there was extremely hard work and very painful, but Colin had not arrived yet, so I either had to wait for him to wheel me down or make my own way to Caroline. I was very self-conscious because I felt the staff could hear and see everything I was saying and doing. I really wanted to talk to Caroline in private but I was in other people's place of work, so privacy was not an option. The midwife looking after Caroline was very friendly and talked to me about how Caroline's night had been. I wasn't really listening; I was too busy having a good look at my baby. I stayed for a while and was able to put my hand into her incubator through the side slot and touch her: she felt warm, but bony.

The midwife asked me if I would like to change her nappy. I said yes, but I was rather apprehensive about hurting her. I got all the bits and pieces together and the midwife left me to it. I removed the old tiny nappy and let out a gasp at what I saw. Caroline had no bottom – just two bones and no fleshy part at all. She also had no labia; they were entirely absent and I could see only the inside parts. I got an awful shock because I had never seen anything like this before and, although Caroline looked emaciated, I hadn't expected her to have no subcutaneous fat anywhere at all. I called the midwife, who told me it was perfectly normal, and that all those bits would grow as Caroline slowly put on weight.

I noticed again that morning that Caroline had no eyelashes or eyebrows either. She did look odd. The midwife explained that Caroline had been taken off the ventilator after only four hours, which was highly encouraging given her size. The CPAP was expected to be left in place for a while longer to be on the safe side, as she had stopped breathing once or twice during the night. All this was normal for a sick and malnourished tiny baby. Caroline's first blood-test results were good, with a haemoglobin level of 19.6 – meaning she had good oxygen-carrying capacity. She also had renal-function tests done, the results of which were perfect. All in all, things were very stable for Caroline. We were reminded continually, however, that small babies can take turns for the worse very quickly and we were by no means out of the woods yet.

A debate began unfolding about whether Caroline might have a short-stature syndrome called Russell–Silver syndrome. Symptoms included a triangular-shaped face and a tendency towards very low blood-sugar levels, or hypoglycaemia. Caroline's face was indeed triangular looking, but anyone who is emaciated has a face that is this shape. The paediatrician who was taking over from our consultant obstetrician decided to put her on tubed fluids with glucose to keep her sugar level high, in case she had this syndrome. In the meantime her bloods were sent for DNA analysis to diagnose whether or not she had it. This tubed-fluid feed was called TPN, but by 28 August she was started on breast milk and at just two days old she was receiving one millilitre of my milk every hour around the clock. It is very important for IUGR babies to be started on foods very slowly as they have adapted to manage on very little in the womb and are not able to tolerate food until they get used to it.

Caroline had also been given precautionary antibodies for a few days in case her immune system was compromised and to reduce the risk of infection. She developed quite bad neonatal jaundice after a few days, which made her look as though she had an amazing tan, but actually neonatal jaundice involves the liver's inability to break down the blood component bilirubin, which builds up, causing this quite attractive colour. Caroline was put on phototherapy, which assists with the removal of these pigments. She had a lamp positioned above her for a few days, shining all the time on her whole body. It worked well and Caroline had the expected pinkness back before long. CPAP was ceased by the end of the second day, and then Caroline was breathing completely on her own.

I noticed on the third day that Caroline's heart rate was much higher than it had been and I mentioned this to the midwife looking after her. She enquired into it and blood was taken for tests. Caroline's blood-sugar levels were getting too high because of all the glucose being pumped into her for fear of complications with Russell–Silver syndrome. I had a feeling then that she did not have that syndrome, and already her emaciated face was beginning to take on a more rounded form. The fluids were stopped immediately and Caroline was put onto breast milk alone. The Russell–Silver syndrome genetic test results came back negative a week later.

During the early days and weeks of Caroline's spell in the neonatal unit, we heard that our consultant visited Caroline virtually every day before his rounds to see how she was and sometimes again in the evenings before he left. This really is testament to the commitment and investment this doctor makes to his patients.

It was slowly dawning on us that Caroline was here and she was doing well, considering everything she had been through. She lost a little weight in the early days, as most babies do, but once her feeding on breast milk commenced, she slowly started putting that back on. Meanwhile I was recovering from the dreaded Caesarean that was not supposed to have happened and expressing breast milk round the clock every four hours. In the first few days a very helpful breast-feeding expert at the hospital sat with me and manually squeezed as much colostrum – the first, antibody-rich secretion from a woman's mammary glands after she gives birth – as she could get out of my breasts. It is a little harder after a Caesarean section to get milk flowing, possibly because of the drugs or the fact the hormones don't kick in as naturally as is the case with a vaginal birth. I never had particularly good levels of colostrum in the first day or two with any of my pregnancies, and my babies would scream the place down with hunger despite being latched onto the breast day and night. Inevitably they would have to receive some formula to drink – despite protestations from the midwives for fear I would not return to breast-feeding, which I always did – until my milk came in and then we would be away. Now, with Caroline, I could physically see how little I was producing and after an hour of quite uncomfortable hand-expressing we had only a few millilitres.

Colostrum is amazing stuff; even small amounts of it are packed full of antibodies to fight infection and the nutrients in the right proportions for a woman's own baby. There was too little milk from me in the first few days to sustain Caroline, so I would rub the colostrum around her dry and cracked lips and smear it round her gums for her to lick and swallow. She had a formula-type supplement to tide her over until my milk came in and when it did – as with all my pregnancies – I could have been feeding a dozen small babies. It was interesting how preciously the midwives treated breast milk, as it was so valuable to them in feeding the small babies – it was often referred to as liquid gold. At one stage, a day or so before I was due to go home, one of the midwives suggested I increase my expressing sessions from four hourly to three hourly to maintain a good supply. This annoyed me, for two reasons. First, Caroline was ingesting only a few millilitres per hour and I was expressing fifty millilitres every four hours; the fridge in the unit was becoming full and I was going to have to start taking some home to my freezer. Second, I was recovering from a major operation – not to mention nine months from hell – and soon I would be fitting the expressing around lengthy journeys into the neonatal unit twice a day to see Caroline, whilst also trying to make up for lost time with my other three children. Each expressing session took up to forty-five minutes, so it was tiring. I felt like saying, 'Get a grip,' or something a little more specific, but I just nodded and ignored the suggestion. I know the suggestion was made in good faith, but it was over the top, I thought.

On the second or third day after Caroline was born Colin and I were able to register her birth and get her birth certificate. This was a hugely emotional and joyful experience because it officially marked her arrival. She now existed as an official person, a new member of the population. Of course, for us she had been a part of our lives for so much longer, but it was exciting to hold the piece of paper that was almost the evidence that she had so far defied all the odds and had arrived – a small but perfect little girl who had really had to fight for her place in the world. We named her Caroline Ann Hamilton. We had no choice about the surname bit – that was Colin's fault! For her first and second names, we debated whether to call her after Colin's mother or mine or any of our grandparents, but we decided not to. Caroline deserved her own identity entirely. She was unique; she was not going to be called after anyone. She was going to have a new name for a new and special life ahead.

After a Caesarean, women normally stay in the hospital for five days. Before I knew it, day five had arrived. My stitches were removed that morning; this was a bit uncomfortable, as the surgeon had chosen to use a single-thread stitch instead of the staples I had had when David was delivered. The staples are a much better idea in my view, because each one can be removed individually and that does not hurt. It looks a bit more savage, but it worked for me. The single stitch, in contrast, was horrible. Blood and fluid had oozed onto it in the previous five days. These had then dried and hardened and the way the stitch was arranged meant it had to be pulled the whole way through from start to finish. Of course, it was stuck four or five times and had to be tugged – as gently as possible – to get it through. It was not massively painful but pinchy and nerve-racking; it was more the idea of the tugging that brought me out in a sweat.

Once my stitches were removed and all my bits and bobs were packed, I had the awful visit to Caroline to say goodbye and leave her in the hospital. I walked down with a heavy heart and sat by her incubator to tell her I would be back soon to see her; I reminded her to be good and that she would be able to come home to our house soon. I tried extremely hard not to cry, but it was futile, and once I started I could not stop. I was in such a bad state the midwives must have rung my ward, because when I did make my way up for the final time they offered me my bed back for a few more days so I wouldn't have to leave Caroline. I declined because I needed to get home to the other children. After almost a year completely revolving around the pregnancy and hospitals and Caroline, they needed me too.

Leaving Caroline was tough, even though I was returning the following morning. Flashes of my three other pregnancies reminded me of the joy of getting out with my gorgeous baby to start life at home. I remembered the little car seat with the baby all snuggled up to make the first journey outside to the car. I wanted to wrap Caroline up and take her with me but I knew it would be some time yet before that would happen. I thanked the staff who had looked after me for so long on the ward – they really had been brilliant. I walked out of the doors with a mixture of relief for me getting out and guilt for Caroline being still stuck inside, and climbed into the car in which my three smiling boys were waiting.

The journey home was just as tough. I felt awful because the boys were so happy to see me and I just could not stop crying. The further we got from the hospital, the worse I got, and I did not want them to think I didn't want to be coming home with them. I explained that I just wanted Caroline to be with us and I think they understood. While they had been home with their dad they had bought a CD for the car, which they loved. It was called *Mums and Dads* and features many of the classics referring to children's relationships with parents. Not the best choice of material to have playing, I would have thought, on that journey, but at the same time it was probably a good idea to get all that raw emotion out rather than leave it bottled up.

One of the songs the boys kept asking for over and over was one about a boy named Luke, who was five and whose dad was Bruce Lee (in his mind) driving him round in his

JCB excavating machine. I have no idea who the artist is but it is a great song. Its message was so clear to me and it was clear why the boys liked hearing it so much: Colin, our boys' dad, had filled the gap very well while I was in hospital and they had formed an amazingly strong bond with him, which remains today. The time Colin spent on his own with the children, as a single parent to all intents and purposes, over the summer weeks brought them closer to each other. For the first time the boys had to rely on Colin for all their needs – from physical to emotional – as I was not available to them except for brief frantic minutes in a bustling antenatal ward in a hospital. With me absent, the home dynamic changed to an all-male domain and all the 'boys stuff' they got up to was much appreciated by the three lads. Nonetheless, anyone who has looked after children will appreciate that this was no mean feat and I know the boys knew that, despite the circumstances, their dad was there for them in every way and that deepened their respect and love for him. Their love of this song was their message over and over again to him in their words, to say, 'We love you and thank you.' I knew I would have to make sure to build up the maternal bonds with them again and ensure they did not think I placed Caroline above them in any way. I was glad I had decided to come home now; ever since that day, when I hear that song, I fill up with tears at the memory of our journey home after nearly six weeks apart.

The summer of 2008 was ending. I had only one more weekend with the boys before school began and I badly wanted to spend it with them. Having arrived home, for a number of days I had the baby blues badly. I felt a need to cry as if to get all the stress and bad experiences out. In the hospital I had cried only that one time when I was so tired and the reaction to that meant I had felt unable to show any emotion from then on for fear they would call a psychiatrist! I think I now had to make up for lost time. The nice thing was that these tears were really tears of joy and relief that our nine months from hell were coming to an end. I did thank God a lot, in case it was he who had intervened for us, or all the prayers my mother and so many others prayed for Caroline. We will never know why she made it, but I like to think it was as much as anything to do with her fighting spirit and will to live, to be with our family and to spend her life with her brothers, Colin and me.

14

LIFE ON THE ROAD TO
SEE CAROLINE

We journeyed to and from the hospital twice a day, most days, and it was very hard. David and Paul were back at school and Samuel had just started playschool. We usually did not make it to the hospital until after ten o'clock in the morning, and we had to be back from the hospital to pick Samuel up at noon. This meant that we did not have a long time to spend with Caroline. On arriving at the hospital, we would go to her incubator. Usually the midwife looking after her would give us a brief account of how she had been overnight and tell us she would get Caroline out for us to hold once she had completed her other duties. This was fine with us, as the staff worked very hard and by now the person minding Caroline was also looking after a few other babies, because Caroline no longer needed one-to-one care. Caroline would be lifted out for us, wires attached, and I would give her kangaroo care – as the name suggests, this involved me 'pouching' her inside my top against my chest. This calmed her; apparently babies thrive when cuddled like this. I imagine the sound of the mother's heartbeat is a throwback to life in the womb; I am surprised Caroline did not react badly, thinking, 'Life wasn't so great in there.'

These were nice times though and it was lovely to feel Caroline's warm body snuggling into her pouch. From early on Caroline was highly alert, was always looking around, and rarely fell asleep when we were there. It was as if she was thinking, 'Sure I'll be asleep the rest of the day.' She was getting visibly bigger by the day; her face was getting prettier and less emaciated-looking. We used to laugh aloud at her cry and the weak, cute little noises she would make in those early days. Colin thought she sounded like a dolphin with a high-pitched sort of squeal, so unlike the boys' baby cries, when she needed something. After a few weeks there were odd items of premature babies' clothes that fit her, so she was dressed and this was far more dignified for her.

Some days when we arrived, if the midwife minding Caroline was busy she would suggest I go to the lactation room and express milk, and she would have Caroline ready when I got back. I used to think this was a very odd request because I would always have expressed in the comfort of my own home before going to the hospital so that my time spent there – all of it – could be with Caroline. I would pick up milk from the freezer on my way in if it was needed for Caroline and it would be thawed out for putting in her syringe to feed her by tube. At some stage in the early weeks one of the midwives asked me to go and express some milk for Caroline as I arrived at the unit. I said I couldn't express as I just had at home and offered to get some frozen milk. She gave me a bit of a lecture to the effect that fresh milk was better for Caroline and told me in future to bring in fresh milk. This had never been raised before, so I was surprised. By now I had lots of stored frozen milk and I was under the impression that with very small babies the milk expressed by the mother changed over time to meet their needs as they grew. For that reason I thought it would be better to give her the earlier milk first and work through the milk until she caught up with her volumes and was on the milk I was producing in real time, as it were. As I had a look at Caroline's notes I noticed the midwife had written that mother (me) was told to bring fresh milk. I did not see the need to put it in writing and felt it was a bit over the top, given that no one else had ever raised it. We decided to ask the paediatrician looking after Caroline and he said it made no difference. Frozen milk, in terms of quality, was very similar to fresh milk and so it was left up to us to decide which batches of my milk Caroline would get.

Occasionally I became involved in what I would call a mini power struggle with the rules of the neonatal unit.

These were about me asserting ownership over my baby. It was hard for me to cope with not having my baby to look after myself. It would be dishonest of me to pretend I was okay with having to ask a midwife to take my baby out for me to hold in the early days, and later to have to ask if I could do it myself. I was an experienced mother. Having held Caroline once or twice, I was very confident about doing things for her. Sometimes having to wait for Caroline to be taken out irritated me, because I would be short of time on the visits. The very fact I had to let someone else do it made me feel inadequate and rather like an aunt instead of a mother. I hated the fact that others fed her, washed her and held her. When I came in I wanted her right away. All these feelings were probably normal but unreasonable, given that these people were doing a great job of bringing Caroline on. As time went by Colin and I were allowed to get Caroline out of the incubator ourselves, but we still had to ask. Being the slight rebel that I am, I gave up on this asking business very quickly and began to assert myself as Caroline's mother. I got the odd glance from the staff, but it was rare that anyone passed any comment when it was noted Caroline was out of her cot without permission.

As time progressed Caroline became less of a priority in the neonatal unit, as much sicker babies arrived, and although I still wanted a blow-by-blow account of what she was up to, this was not really happening, given her improved condition and the busy state of the unit on most days. It was possibly unfair of me to expect the minute details, as within a week or two she was out of immediate danger and perhaps the staff felt I did not need to know everything that was happening. The problem was that I did. Because I was acutely conscious of how busy staff were, I had taken to not hassling them with questions. Instead I spent a little time every visit reading Caroline's notes. I assumed there was no issue with doing this as Caroline could not read them herself and so it would be fine for me, as her mother and legal guardian, to do that. I did again get the occasional glance from the staff as I read her previous day's medical history, but I assumed this was because most other parents did not feel the need to do this and so it was unusual. For at least two or three weeks, nothing was ever said to me regarding this, and most staff knew reading Caroline's notes was something I did routinely when I visited. It did not seem to be a problem.

However, one day as I was having my usual read of the notes while Colin had his cuddle with Caroline, a midwife came over to me and said I wasn't allowed to read Caroline's notes and asked me to stop. I asked her what she meant. She said I was entitled to have the notes read and explained to me with a midwife present but was not allowed access to them myself. I asked her why and she explained it was because parents might read something they didn't understand and panic. I replied that I thought that was unlikely, as if parents did not understand something they would ask, not fly off into a panic.

She continued by saying that there was no need to read the notes anyway because the midwives passed on any relevant changes or issues when the parents visited. Now in my view this part just was not accurate. There were many things I had read in Caroline's notes that I considered relevant but that we were never told, such as about the routine and regular tests carried out for MRSA (the hospital superbug). The results for Russell–Silver syndrome had been back for days, and appeared in the notes before they were mentioned to us. Now I am not complaining about that at all, because the staff were so busy and, with continual changeover of shifts we couldn't possibly be informed of everything; but this was why it seemed ideal to be checking things myself daily and only asking questions where appropriate.

It was probably not the policy that irked me, but this midwife's attitude. Other staff were either unaware of the policy or were willing to turn a blind eye and let me look at the notes on my own. I didn't see the need for this person not to do likewise. Clearly my hormones had not yet settled down and I went into a major rant. I explained to the midwife that it was I who had carried Caroline through the ups and downs of a rotten pregnancy; I who had spent the majority of the summer in the hospital so that she would be safe; I who had listened to awful predictions that she might not make it; and I who was expressing milk for her night and day and trying to manage family life without her at home. I told the midwife I would not compete with hospital staff for total and complete access to my baby's records and reminded her in no uncertain terms that I, not she, was Caroline's mother. I told her they could finish looking after Caroline for as long as was necessary and ring me when she was ready to come home, as I was not playing second fiddle to the unit any more. I marched out with poor Colin, who did not know what to say or do, and I left without even getting to say goodbye to Caroline.

It is only fair to note here that the midwife came after me and apologised, but for me the damage was done. I just could not take being reprimanded after everything I had been through. Later that day one of the managers called, having presumably been told the story, and in a clear and conciliatory way explained the policy and asked me to keep coming in as it was so important to Caroline's development. I said I would, and apologised for the outburst. The manager made it clear that the midwives would sit down and go through the notes with us every day, as we were entitled to see them. I said that would be fine. I take significant responsibility for this incident, as I was struggling with almost a year of continual stress and unknowns and had a strong instinct to take control of Caroline's welfare myself.

I was tired of being a 'pseudomother', which is how I felt while Caroline was in hospital. These were my issues, not the neonatal unit's. I do appreciate that now.

As the days went on I would ask the midwife minding Caroline to go through the notes with me when a chance arose. I felt awful because the midwives were so busy, but I wanted the details on her feeds, her haemoglobin levels and, of course, any tests being done on her. For a few days whichever midwife was on duty would go through the notes. The midwives had obviously heard the news about my rant. However, before long they would start going through the notes and then say they had to do something quickly and I could have a quick look myself and when they were back I could clarify anything I needed to with them. I took this action to be in support of me. One or two staff did say they would want full access to their child's details at any time without someone having to go through the details with them. It was a way around the policy: technically someone was going through the notes, but in an on-and-off fashion. This suited me and I felt less guilty about taking up too much of the staff's time. Looking back, I think the reaction was another little power or control thing. Again, the incident was between one individual and one very hormonal mother, so who knows what was really meant by it all? It was just one of those things that set me off during Caroline's lengthy stay in the neonatal unit.

I myself was recovering slowly as the weeks passed. Within a few days of going home I had to go back into the hospital for a scan as I developed heavy bleeding and cramping. I had a most unusual scan this time. Because I had the Caesarean scar, which was still very sore, I couldn't have the normal transducer – part of the scanning equipment – pushed over my stomach, as was usual, to take a look inside the womb. Instead, a horrendous-looking instrument, like a big white penis, was inserted into my vagina to see the womb. I had never seen anything like it! It did the trick, however, revealing that there was no major problem, just a slight infection. I was put on antibiotics and went home.

With David, years before, my Caesarean scar had healed quickly after the stitches. The scar was trickier this time: there was one small section, to the right of the scar, that kept opening and bleeding. I was terrified it would become infected, so I paid a lot of attention to it. It took nearly six weeks to seal fully, I am sure due to the travelling in and out to the hospital on bumpy roads, the fact this was a second Caesarean section, and my being much older. But the scar did heal eventually and I was getting physically stronger. I needed to be, as I had signed up for a Master of Education degree earlier in the year and just two weeks after delivering Caroline I started lectures. I remember still being in a lot of pain getting back and forth and finding it hard to concentrate on the course and on Caroline. At the same time, the course was a great way for me to take my mind off everything and think of something different for a change. As the weeks went by, I would bring coursework or reading into the hospital with me and sit beside Caroline's cot while she slept, doing a little bit of work while still spending time with her.

Caroline's move from the intensive-care section to the high-dependency section took about two weeks. One day I arrived with my mother and was excited to see that Caroline was now in high dependency. Another morning I recall vividly occurred just days after Caroline was moved out of intensive care. I arrived at the unit to find Caroline screaming in her incubator. Her heart rate was soaring and she was sweating all over. There was no sign of her midwife, who may have been on a break. Having just arrived, I had no idea whether Caroline might be hungry or in pain and I looked around for another midwife. There was only one other baby in the high-dependency section that day and I figured the same midwife was looking after both babies. There was probably another midwife from intensive care or special care to keep an eye on Caroline and the other baby, but this midwife was busy elsewhere. Since Caroline was getting hysterical, I decided to get her out but she wouldn't calm down. I wondered if she was due a feed; I wasn't allowed to syringe feed her on my own, so after a few seconds I decided I would try to breastfeed her. Caroline had never been tried with a bottle or the breast and was still on tube feeds. I latched her on as I had done with my three boys and without any trouble or fuss at all she began sucking. The reflex was fully there and she settled in for a cuddle and a feed. I was so thrilled to be able to soothe her and to realise there might be no need to keep tube feeding her if she could feed on her own.

The midwife arrived back a while later and was very surprised to find Caroline out of her incubator, let alone feeding happily. I could see she was in two minds about whether to say anything about my actions, so before she had a chance to do so I got in first, explaining that Caroline had been distressed and, as I did not know where the midwife was, I had fed her. After all, it was the most natural thing in the world for a mother to do for her child. The midwife could hardly object; I could not have left Caroline distressed. From that day on Caroline was weaned off her tube, and her bottle feeds increased steadily. This was a great move forward for Colin and me on a number of levels. First, it meant that we could do a lot more of the hands-on work. We were able to ring and check when Caroline was due a feed and leave a message that we would be in to do that feed. It meant that we became the most consistent people she saw and we often wondered whether she was beginning to know us. We found it difficult to tell.

Caroline was getting very beautiful by the day. The small

red birthmarks were fading and her skin was taking on a lovely glow. Her little cheeks were filling out and her eyes were open and bright. She had a new woolly hat on every few days, thanks to a lady who took it upon herself to knit extra-small hats for the unit's babies. I realised what a small world we live in when I returned to work to discover this lady too was now working there. It was wonderful to meet and thank her.

Within a few days of arriving in the high-dependency section, Caroline was in an open cot and the staff were testing whether she was able to regulate her own temperature. She managed to do so without any difficulty at all; we knew after four weeks that really all Caroline had to do now was grow and continue to feed well in order to get home. We met the consultant who had looked after her as we were leaving the hospital one day. We talked about how amazing it was that a baby who had had to be delivered as an emergency at just twenty-eight weeks, whose mother had been in the antenatal ward with me, was the very same weight as Caroline, who was born a full nine weeks later. This baby grew at the same rate as Caroline and seemed to follow her from intensive care to high dependency to special care. It was amazing, too, that Caroline could be so far behind her gestational weight and yet we still had no idea what had gone wrong. At that point we were too busy focusing on getting Caroline well and home.

The diary I kept from Caroline's notes showed she was making great progress. Table 2 shows her growth over the six weeks she was in the neonatal unit.

Table 2: Caroline's growth over the six weeks she was in the neonatal unit

Date	Weight in kilograms	Weight in pounds and ounces
26 August	Birth weight: 1.18 kg	2 lb 9 oz
28 August	Weight fell to 1.13 kg	2 lb 7 oz
31 August	Weight unchanged at 1.13 kg	2 lb 7 oz
3 September	Weight up to 1.19 kg	2 lb 10 oz
6 September	Weight up to 1.22 kg	2 lb 11 oz
11 September	Weight up to 1.29 kg	2 lb 13 oz
14 September	Weight up to 1.36 kg	3 lb
18 September	Weight up to 1.47 kg	3 lb 4 oz
21 September	Weight up to 1.54 kg	3 lb 7 oz
25 September	Weight up to 1.68 kg	3 lb 11 oz
28 September	Weight up to 1.77 kg	3 lb 14 oz
2 October	Weight up to 1.88 kg	4 lb 2 oz
5 October	Weight up to 1.97 kg	4 lb 5 oz

15

CAROLINE PREPARES TO COME HOME

As Caroline's growth in the neonatal unit (see Table 2) indicates, once feeding became well established, Caroline began to gain weight quite quickly, almost doubling her birth weight within six weeks. It was amazing that, whereas there had been many weeks when Caroline was in the womb that she had only grown a single ounce, now she was being fed only breast milk she was still managing to grow by up to seven ounces most weeks. From 4 September, a fortifier was added to her breast milk to add calories. I was instructed to tip away the first third of all breast milk I expressed because it was the watery part to quench thirst – the latter half had the fat. I let on that I did this, but often I didn't, because I felt if it was being produced it was needed, and I was worried she would be thirsty with the fortifier and only the fatty part of the breast milk. I was not in the same mad rush as I sometimes felt the doctors were to put weight on Caroline. She had managed for a long time on very little and I knew she was the kind of baby who would now grow at her own rate. I didn't want to put pressure on her gut or force-feed her, as it were, although I knew the sooner she put weight on the sooner she would be able to come home and, I hoped, begin to thrive.

The only other medicines Caroline received whilst in the unit were antibiotics at the start because her umbilical cord looked a little infected, and she was also on extra iron and vitamins. By 23 September Caroline's haemoglobin had dropped from 19 at birth to 11.6; it had fallen further to 10.8 by 29 September. There was a concern that if it fell any lower she might need a blood transfusion as another premature baby had recently done. The haemoglobin settled, however, and there was no need to intervene. On 30 September Caroline was diagnosed with a slight heart murmur. This was worrying, as I didn't really know much about murmurs. It turned out it was very slight, so much so that the doctors sometimes could not even hear it. It was termed an innocent murmur or a flow murmur, meaning there was no indication there was any potential heart problem, but that Caroline's heart sounds were slightly more audible than usual. Sometimes it would be there and sometimes not; there was nothing to worry about.

On 2 October, whilst in the special-care section awaiting a date of release, a woman whose baby had been born prematurely, but at a much higher birth weight than Caroline's, received some terrible news. Her baby had had a routine cranial ultrasound because she was due to go home, and this had discovered brain damage. The baby was feeding and growing well and appeared perfect, but was going to have some disability. The extent of the damage was not clear and wouldn't be until the child was older. The hardest thing to bear about this story was that the woman found out only hours before she was due to leave. One minute she thought she was bringing a perfectly healthy baby home, and the next she was told her baby had suffered a bleed on the brain, which had caused the damage. Colin and I felt deeply for her, as we had become acquaintances over the weeks. We told her of the predictions some doctors had made about Caroline's prospects and encouraged her to try to put the prediction of brain damage out of her mind and to see what would happen. We searched through Caroline's notes that day for any mention of a cranial ultrasound. It emerged this test is done based on degree of prematurity, not birth weight, and so Caroline had not been tested. I remember our consultant saying, whenever I asked him, that Caroline's brain looked structurally fine on the scans, but I wanted to be sure it had stayed that way. We asked if Caroline could be checked; given her low birth weight, the hospital staff agreed. Luckily the test results were fine; this was another big hurdle crossed.

We were luckier than many in that we had a friend working in the neonatal unit. If there was ever anything bothering us or anything we wanted to query we could ask her. She had been there for us throughout the pregnancy, and we appreciated her expertise and friendship.

Our time in the special-care unit followed the period in the high-dependency unit. Once Caroline had proven she could regulate her own temperature, she was finally shifted to the special-care room into which I had glanced wistfully all those weeks before when I visited the unit. It was hard to believe Caroline was at this final stage before going home. Life in special care was good preparation for going home. Midwives here often had a number of babies to feed and care for, as most were no longer sick, and any help parents could give with their own baby was now appreciated.

Caroline was approaching the six-week-old mark and getting her personality by now. I remember a few of the midwives mentioning she was making herself known to them; I assume she was demanding more attention as she got older. Caroline was no longer too keen on the idea of sleep, eat and sleep again. She was beginning to whinge when she was put back in her cot, wanting to be picked up again. While I thought this was just the best news ever, the midwives, who had many other babies to tend to, did not. We made an extra effort at this stage to spend longer with Caroline. We used to laugh a little, however, when Caroline

– fed and changed and snuggled up, looking as though she might nod off – would let us get only as far as the door before, realising she was being left, starting to whinge. The midwives would say, 'Leave her and she will be okay.' Whereas I definitely would have done this with the boys, there was no way on Earth this little one was going to suffer any more than she had already. In I would go again and walk around with her, showing her whatever I could to tire her, although the place is designed to be peaceful for sleep and there wasn't much for her to see. I had been doing this for a few days and one of the midwives we hadn't met before had noticed it. I think she had sympathised with Caroline's story and was fond of her. She felt that Caroline was desperate for stimulation. We talked about what we could do. The staff were far too busy to play much with the babies, and Colin and I could spend only a limited amount of time with Caroline. This midwife said I could bring in a baby bouncer, which we had at home, so that after a feed Caroline could watch the staff at work and the comings and goings in the unit. She also agreed to get permission for us to bring some colourful toys to attach to Caroline's cot, so she could watch them while lying down.

We bought her a colourful tiger, with noisy materials on him for touching, and a rattle-like toy for across the cot. It was hilarious the first time she spotted the tiger. She was whingeing to be picked up, with her eyes half open, and as she turned there was this mad colourful tiger looking in the Perspex side of her cot. She immediately stopped whingeing and looked at it with wide eyes. We weren't sure whether she would howl or not, but she just kept staring at it, and it seemed to do the trick in stimulating her.

After her feed that day we put her in the bouncer as we prepared to leave. That was very funny too. Caroline was still so small that the strap that holds the baby in the bouncer was right across her eyes, completely blocking her view of anything. We had to prop her up with blankets so that she could just about peer out over the top of it. Everyone who came in was in stitches at the sight of her sitting up and looking around her in awe at the world from a new angle.

Just when there was talk of Caroline coming home she developed the snuffles – either a cold or a drying out of her nasal passages due to the warm air in the neonatal unit. She was not able to feed as well as normal, as her ability to breathe while she sucked the bottle was impaired. She was given saline drops and she improved. The snuffles happened again, however, and this time no one seemed to treat it or even notice it. There was a time when staff did talk about putting her feeding tube back in because she was slow taking her feeds, but the blocked nose wasn't being taken into account. We didn't really know to what extent it was affecting her feeds, but knew if she went back on the tube she would remain in the hospital for ages. The midwife who had negotiated the toys for Caroline saw me struggling to feed her one day, and asked if she could take over. She watched as Caroline fed and she could see Caroline was still totally blocked. She got a contraption like a suction tube attached to a machine and removed a load of mucus from her nasal passages. Caroline finished the bottle much more quickly. She wrote a note for all midwives that before every feed Caroline was to be suctioned, or at least have saline drops administered to break up or clear mucus, and her feeds improved.

We began pushing at that point to bring her home, but because of the slight feeding blip the doctors were somewhat reluctant. This midwife challenged them one day, repeating what she had already expressed to us: Caroline had reached the point where the neonatal unit could do no more for her. The midwife believed Caroline's progress could now be enhanced only by getting her home to the stimulation of family life. She felt Caroline needed far more attention than the unit could offer her, and she very clearly expressed the view that Caroline should be allowed home. The paediatrician conceded that if Caroline fed well for a further forty-eight hours he would let her home. This was a huge challenge as she was still quite snuffly, but everyone made an effort and Caroline was signed off to go home on 8 October, exactly six weeks and one day after she had been born. Her discharge weight was 4 lb 7 oz (2.02 kg), a big improvement from 2 lb 9 oz (1.18 kg) but still tiny.

The morning on which she was due to leave, Colin and I took some clothes from home to the hospital for Caroline to wear for the first time. The boys came in with us and we had a lovely picture taken all together, ready to take our baby home at last. The boys thought Caroline looked cute and funny in the red baby's car-seat they had all used. At home, many pictures and welcome-home cards were ready for her to look at. It was a very strange feeling walking out of the doors of the neonatal unit: I don't really know what I felt. The staff there had done so much for Caroline, especially the midwife who had been instrumental in getting her home. I felt huge gratitude for the interest beyond the job that this midwife gave us. There were so many other people, too, who had helped – from doctors, consultants and midwives to counsellors, friends and family. Together they had made Caroline's survival possible and helped Colin and me through it all.

I didn't look back, however; I got out as fast as I could before the hospital staff changed their minds. I said, 'Thank God,' as I walked out of the main hospital doors, and vowed I would not have another baby. This was it: we had a fabulous family. We felt extremely lucky that Caroline had come so far relatively unscathed. We knew there were going to be many more appointments and check-ups to try to find out if anything was genetically wrong with Caroline and to see if she would continue improving. But none of that was going to be any tougher than what we had already been through. I didn't look back as the car pulled out of the hospital car park but said a silent 'Thank you' to all the people there who had shown us kindness. We are grateful to each and every one of them.

16

REAL FAMILY LIFE
BEGINS AGAIN

Caroline slept all the way home during her first time in a car, as all my other children had done. When we got home, she stayed asleep for ages. Of course, we were all dying for her to wake up so we could be with her and show her around. We were determined to do everything we could to stimulate her, as I was very conscious that developmentally she had not experienced the same first six weeks other babies had. We probably overdid it with the poor child! Between books and toys, and talking and whizzing children all around her, she didn't know what had hit her, I'd say. I remember her loving the dancing flames of the fire, which we lit daily, even though it was only early October, because the hospital had been so warm we were terrified she would be cold or uncomfortable. We took her to our local general practitioner and his nurse within a few days of coming home. In the early stages of the pregnancy I had been there often for my routine check-ups, but as time had gone by I had been seen only at the hospital. Nonetheless they had both been supportive during the pregnancy and were pleased to see Caroline at last. The GP was keen that we keep an eye on the volume of milk Caroline was taking, just in case her weight gain fell away now she was out of the hospital and living a normal life.

Her first day of feeds was recorded on 15 October; she had seven feeds in twenty-four hours. The volumes she was taking ranged from thirty millilitres to fifty-five millilitres (from one to two ounces). This was still very little but Caroline weighed only 4 lb 7 oz, so she was doing quite well. Within four days her feeds were still at seven in twenty-four hours, but they were now ranging from forty millilitres to eighty millilitres, so her capacity to feed was improving steadily. Her weight continued to rise, with a climb from 4 lb 7 oz (2.02 kg) coming home to 5 lb 3 oz (2.4 kg) three weeks later.

We were all very happy, even though getting up at night was busy for Colin and me. I would express a feed and Colin would bottle-feed Caroline a previously expressed bottle. It was non-stop for both of us, but we were determined to enjoy every minute and we did, despite the tiredness. We talked a lot those nights. I would laugh when Colin said he was tired, and even though I was too, I thought it was a piece of cake compared to life in hospital. Colin talked a lot about the evenings when he had taken an extra trip to the hospital to see Caroline while I had stayed home with the other children. He told me lots of things he hadn't mentioned before, for example how, if she was upset, Caroline would totally calm down, in terms of breathing and heart rate on her monitors, when he laid his hands right over her whole body. It was like a form of reiki or something similar: she would respond to his touch and, even though she might have been half asleep, she knew he was there. He loved their time together because he knew that when she came home I would be the one doing most of the hands-on caring. Despite all the medical intervention so necessary to get Caroline better, we were both able to develop close bonds with Caroline, which are still strong today. It was nice to have that time at night, when the other children were sleeping, to go over everything again together. I suppose it was a form of therapy for us to come to terms with what had happened and to be thankful for the happy outcome; we knew well that not everyone was as lucky.

Caroline was a slow and often reluctant feeder, however. I would never, ever, refer to her as a hungry baby, which is how I would have described my boys. She could take or leave food. She rarely woke up crying for a feed and guzzling the bottle like other babies do. This is normal behaviour for severe IUGR babies; it is a battle to feed them. I'd imagine this is due to their having coped for so long with a scarce supply of food, or else because their appetite development is hampered by starvation in the womb. We had to become good at finding ways to keep Caroline drinking, for example by tickling her toes or under her chin to stimulate her to swallow. We always managed to get the feed into her, but it did require fierce commitment at times. By 21 October I was sick and tired of having to express every feed and then feed Caroline. Each session could take up to an hour and a half, and it seemed ridiculous, when Caroline was doing so well, to keep this up. I began replacing a bottle feed with a breast feed, but I did it very slowly in case Caroline stopped gaining weight: first one bottle, followed by two, over a period of many weeks. Caroline continued to grow despite our now not having any idea how much she was actually getting during the breast feeds, as we couldn't measure these. By Sunday 16 November – at eleven weeks old and five weeks out of the hospital – Caroline was being fully breastfed and enjoying it. We were both much more relaxed and happy. Gone were the days of expressing, sterilising, thawing milk and heating bottles; Caroline could just feed whenever and wherever she needed to. Nights became easier too, as I could rest more and didn't have the worry that I would wake the other children with the awful noise of the breast pump.

Caroline had a fair few appointments in those early weeks. First she had vaccinations; these were even worse than normal because it was stressful seeing a baby so small being injected and hurt by a needle, and because we didn't know if she would react differently because of her size. There was no difference at all, however; she had no high temperatures or side effects of any description. Her eyes needed to be checked for retinopathy, a disease of the retina – the light-sensitive region of the eye – and a common side effect of prematurity or, presumably, low birthweight. The retinopathy tests were not pleasant either: she had silver instruments put on her eyelids to hold them open and stop her blinking while special drops were inserted. This allowed a good view of the retina to be examined. Luckily both her eyes were perfect apart from blocked tear ducts, which was only a minor issue that our other children had all had, so that was another worry out of the way. We did take Caroline to the GP on one occasion as we had noticed, on numerous visits to the neonatal unit, that she was inclined to jitter (that's what we called it): she shook in a startled sort of way if she was agitated. It never happened when she was asleep. I was concerned it might be a condition called 'essential tremors', which can be a lifelong problem (I researched this on the internet again), but it turned out to be common in smaller babies. It is some sort of exaggerated startle reflex that usually settles down with time. It did disappear at some point – I don't remember when – or we just stopped noticing it.

Probably the toughest thing about Caroline – apart from the worry that at some stage we would get news that she did in fact have some nasty gene-related condition that would hold her back – was her ability to not sleep. I am aware that this is a worldwide issue with many children, regardless of their start in life, but with Caroline it was new for us. Having been so lucky with three boys who were brilliant sleepers from early on, we found it a huge adaptation to have a baby who could manage on so little sleep. From the early days it was understandable that she needed to make up for lost feeding time in the womb, but her sleep never really improved hugely. I think she got used to being cuddled a lot and, of course, slept in my arms during the day, so maybe we gave her bad habits. She definitely kept us on our toes day and night, but actually we didn't really care. We knew (hoped) at some stage she would sleep through the night in her own time. I used to imagine she was telling me, when she gurgled in the dead of night, awake and wanting to play, that she had had more than enough sleep in the neonatal unit for six weeks to do any girl at least a full year.

We were extremely fortunate to have a brilliant public-health nurse when we got home. She had worked in the neonatal unit and was highly familiar with premature and small-for-gestational-age babies. I am not sure whether she was asked to do so or not, but this nurse visited Caroline to check on her progress every week for two months after we had brought her home, then fortnightly for a few months, until finally the visits were only required monthly up to Caroline's first birthday. She was very pleasant and extremely fond of Caroline. What I loved about her was that she was convinced Caroline was just an IUGR baby and never really entertained the possibility of any other syndrome or other problem. It wasn't that she kept saying, 'There's nothing wrong with this one,' or anything like that; it was how she treated her. She had weekly access to Caroline's development, and I think she saw nothing in it that was not normal. She used to marvel at what Caroline could do for her age, given her size, and always said how amazing she was. She heard us mention that it was thought Caroline possibly had some unusual facial features, but she always felt Caroline just had the look of a premature baby. There must be a characteristic look – common to premature or very small babies – with which she was familiar. She was instrumental in encouraging me to move to full-time breastfeeding, as she could see Caroline was doing well and knew it was hard going for me trying to express and feed. I remember her always being in good form and cheery, which was wonderful because we saw her a lot and it would have been tough if she had been an odd sort of character. We were never properly able to say a big thank you to her, because the visits fizzled out when we received a letter telling us to go to the local clinic for one of Caroline's checks; we then realised Caroline was back in the normal system at last, which was great. She was a wonderful, friendly, professional nurse and we are very grateful for the work she did with Caroline.

Caroline's growth continued steadily for the remainder of her first year. We took her to the paediatrician twice a year to see how she was doing. Caroline seemed to grow at her own rate and did not exhibit much catch up, but was still healthy and doing well. By her first birthday, which despite some predictions she did make and enjoyed thoroughly, as did the family, she had added more than 3.94 inches (10 centimetres) to her head circumference. Her height had increased from 16.15 inches (41 centimetres) at birth to 25.61 inches (65 centimetres) at one year. Her weight was doing the least well of all the measurements on the growth charts, but it had increased five-fold, going from 2 lb 9 oz (1.18 kg) to almost 14 lb (6.35 kg). To us this was amazing in such a short time.

I think when the doctors saw her weight at one year they really did not remember how small she actually was at full term, when she was born. They would have liked to see her bigger, as we all would have and still would, but she is still very young and has plenty of time. Now, with Caroline three years old, when we look back at her measurements, it is still shocking to see that she was already six months old, on solids and sitting up, when she reached nine pounds – the weight at which her brothers Paul and Samuel were born. Her weight at one year was the weight her brothers were at their six-week check-up. But it is all relative: they weren't starved in the womb and they didn't have to fight for survival. Even though they are bigger than her, she is well able to slap them down to size.

A special day in Caroline's first year was her christening. It marked her joining of a community, her being alive. She was our first to be christened in our local church as we had moved a few miles since the boys were born. Her Irish granny and granddad were present, as was her Scottish granny. Sadly, her granddad had passed away only a few short months after she had been born. He had known that she was born and well before he died, however, and this had meant a lot to him. My two brothers, their wives and our children's one Irish cousin came along to join the celebration with our family that day. As usual, Caroline made her presence known by refusing to feed all morning and giving everyone trouble, but she did behave impeccably for the ceremony. The local priest did not know Caroline's history but said some lovely words, and we had a good day.

Caroline surprised no one by starting to roll around, despite her diminutive frame, by eight months – and I mean really rolling around. No toy was unreachable; she could manoeuvre in every direction to get it. She was crawling at ten months, and we have some wonderful video footage of her grunting and groaning with the determination to get up on all fours and move her knees underneath her. She used to stick her tongue out in total concentration as she practised over and over again until she got moving. By her first birthday party, during which she was in her element as the centre of attention, she was pushing a walking-frame toy around, using it as support. We had to take her out of the actual walker infants sit in and use their legs to propel, as she would deliberately run it towards our ankles and ram us whenever she got the chance. She was lethal: she would try to run it down single steps to get out, which was getting dangerous. By fourteen months she was fully mobile. I will never forget her giggling when she was managing to take those early steps on her own, before falling over. Sometimes she was laughing so hysterically she would fall down and have to calm herself to have another go. Of course, the shouts of encouragement from the boys, Colin and me could be heard in the next county, and that really got her going. All her teeth arrived exactly on time, which was surprising, as we didn't know if they would be delayed because of her size.

Caroline's first year, in terms of health, was excellent, which I put down partly to her being breastfed to some degree until she was eleven months old. She did get chicken pox at the same time as Samuel, for which she needed some antiviral medication, as it was quite a severe dose. She had no coughs or colds for the period she was being breastfed, but during her second and third winters she did have a lot of chest infections and quite a few antibiotics. She has to develop her own immunity; we are told that until she reaches the middle centiles for her weight she will continue to be susceptible to infection. She has had only one hospitalisation in nearly three years, due to a virus. She wouldn't drink because of the high temperatures it caused, and she became dehydrated.

Now, at three years old, she sees a dietician who has put her on a high-calorie milk to supplement her intake and ensure she is getting all the nutrients and iron she needs, as her appetite is quite poor some days. She is at the stage where playing and running around are of more interest to her than eating is, and of course all the activity makes it difficult to keep weight on her – she is so good at burning it off. This remains our biggest challenge, and the fact she still decides not to sleep well some nights. I know there are other children with the same problem, but this knowledge doesn't, of course, make it any easier for us. She does possibly have asthma, but so did two of her brothers, and if she does we hope she will grow out of it; it could just be frequent chest infections, and is not definite yet. Overall, Caroline is a very active little girl who is still fighting back after a very tough start in life and very much winning the battle, I would say. If we had had a clear diagnosis as Caroline progressed to this point, this might have helped us explain some of her challenges with immunity, feeding and sleep, but in a way 'no news was good news'. Without any definite answers, we could pretend Caroline was a perfectly healthy young girl.

17

THE SEARCH
FOR ANSWERS

Although we had no definite answers about Caroline's condition as she passed her first and second birthdays and headed towards her third, the search for them was always ongoing. When Caroline was ten weeks old we received a letter inviting us to meet a geneticist who was asked by the hospital to have a look at Caroline. We had been told that he was excellent at his job and had a formal approach to consultations. We were advised to listen and ask questions, but to be polite at all times. Maybe by now my reputation as a bit of an incessant questioner preceded me, and the hospital staff thought I would upset the geneticist. I was a little nervous about meeting him, but both Colin and I found him pleasant, with a wicked, somewhat sarcastic, sense of humour – quite dry, but he would make us grin. I got the distinct impression he didn't suffer fools gladly, and I could imagine he would put us in our place if it was required. However, he has been so good to us and Caroline that we cannot think of anything that hasn't been positive in meeting him. For instance, when we first met him his opening comment was, 'So this is the little lady who has skipped all the queues to be seen by me.' I told him that it must have been the hospital that had done that, just in case he thought we were making demands, but I think he knew this was the case already. At that first consultation he gave Caroline a thorough examination and we talked about the pregnancy and everything that had happened. He did a pedigree study, covering any familial details, unusual conditions or deaths noted.

At the end of this consultation he mentioned a syndrome called Robinow, which we hadn't come across. It is a short-stature syndrome, with growth restricted equally in limbs, trunk and head. I remember the geneticist mentioning that it would not be the worst syndrome she could have as it didn't impact to any great degree on intellectual development. He made it clear that since Caroline was so young and her features were still developing, this diagnosis of Robinow syndrome may not turn out to be definitive, as there was no official test. Instead, there was mainly clinical diagnosis with some radiological assistance. He was impressed with Caroline's early development, as she was alert, holding her head up and really taking everything in, and he felt her feeding and growth were satisfactory. Caroline then had to have a full skeletal survey done, which was hard. She had to have X-rays taken of her hands, feet, vertebral column, skull – the whole lot. It was difficult to isolate the parts of the body that were being X-rayed on a tiny baby who was wriggling and deeply unimpressed with the cold, hard surface of the X-ray bed. I remember the staff putting the tiniest little lead apron on her nappy region to protect her ovaries. The woman actually taking the tests seemed unsure of how to proceed with placing Caroline for the different shots. I was becoming very stressed because I didn't know either, and Caroline was showing increasing distress as the time passed. Eventually all the X-rays were complete and we had to head down to the sections where bloods were taken. Again poor Caroline had to have a vein found and have a quantity of her blood squeezed manually into vials, which took a while. By now she was hysterical, and I wasn't feeling much better myself. I felt so sorry for her having to go through more pain, but I knew it was for the best and was necessary to find the underlying cause of Caroline's condition.

The following year we met the geneticist again. A paediatrician was also present, and again Caroline had a thorough examination. The bone X-rays showed that Caroline's bone age was far behind her actual age. Other than that, we gathered, the bone X-rays appeared normal and it was felt this situation would resolve itself to some degree as Caroline got older. Again, there were comments that Caroline was making excellent progress developmentally, which was reassuring. The X-rays were to be sent to another country to be checked. At this appointment the geneticist seemed less sure about Robinow, as Caroline's facial features were changing very significantly as she grew. There were other syndromes to look into, and he took a photo of Caroline, saying he would call us back the following spring. At this appointment Caroline's heart murmur was heard again, and it was decided she would attend a specialist to have it checked out in case of a problem. The geneticist was very pleased with Caroline's physical development, but would have liked, I think, to see her catching up on the growth curves a little more quickly.

Caroline was eighteen months old when the geneticist next saw her. By now she was stringing two or more words together, which was a good sign. She was running around and very steady on her feet, as she had been walking since she was fourteen months old. She was funny at this appointment: she wanted everything on the desk she could get her hands on and was approaching the terrible twos attitudinally, which meant she wasn't taking no for an answer. She demanded to be up when she was down and down when she was up. I remember the geneticist casually mentioning that she was turning into a proper little madam, and I couldn't but agree with him. It was great to see her feisty independence emerging.

By now the geneticist was looking only at syndromes with normal intelligence, as it was clear Caroline was doing very well developmentally. Her height and head size were still not improving at the rate he would have liked, but there was no immediate cause for concern. There were no further developments in terms of a possible syndrome, but Caroline, Colin and I did all have blood taken so that a profile of our DNA could be examined, and probably compared, to check for various scenarios. It was at this appointment that I was asked if our family was complete. I smirked as I had only recently mentioned to Colin almost joking that we could have one more. I replied that it was more than likely that I would not want more children and that Colin definitely didn't. The geneticist reminded me that I was in my fortieth year, to which I replied that I had only just turned thirty-nine. He reiterated that I was indeed in my fortieth year and explained the risks of something going wrong generally at that age. He explained, too, that because we didn't have a firm diagnosis for Caroline there could well be further genetic risks if she were to have a genetic problem passed on from either Colin or me. He was very nice, however, and I felt as though we could be ourselves with him, as we were getting to know him. I think Caroline was working her charms on him too and I like to think, despite her being his patient, he was fond of her.

We met the geneticist again one year later. Although he was still concerned about Caroline's growth, he explained to us that the top bone experts in the world had examined her X-rays and that the European Skeletal Dysplasia Network had found absolutely no evidence of bone abnormality beyond that of severe IUGR. I was elated at that news and glad to have official confirmation that Caroline's bones were normal. It didn't mean that a short-stature syndrome was out of the question but Caroline was almost diagnosed as a 'normal' healthy child with no condition beyond the side effects of IUGR. The geneticist decided, however, to do another set of blood tests and have a look at one more syndrome: Floating–Harbor syndrome, which is characterised by short stature and delayed bone age at birth, and which also has implications for development of expressive speech and some unusual facial features. Before we left, Caroline marched up to the geneticist and said in her most polite voice, 'Doctor, where is my sticker?' (pronounced 'dicker' as she wasn't very good at 's' yet). He smiled and gave her some spiel about the fact he wasn't prone to bribery, unlike the outgoing government, and, as she walked away wholly unimpressed by the lack of a sticker, he commented in a most genuine tone that she was a delightful child and that we were very lucky. The message wasn't lost on us: we were fortunate not only to have a lovely child but also one who was doing very well in every way, despite her shockingly low birth weight at full term. It was nice to hear this and it is true: Caroline is lovely and special, and we are so blessed to have her with us. We will never take that for granted.

In July 2011, we unexpectedly received a call, followed by a letter, to say that the geneticist had found something on the latest set of Caroline's tests and he would like to see us both with Caroline within weeks. We all met with him in August 2011 to receive the first definitive reasons for Caroline's unexplained growth restriction. He explained that Caroline has a condition known as uniparental disomy. I was familiar with this scenario from previous reading and my general interest in genetics as a biology teacher. My interpretation from his description of the condition was that at some stage in Caroline's conception or very early development she had a large section of chromosome 22 from either Colin or me that either was deleted after conception or absent from the egg or sperm initially through some, probably spontaneous, mutation in the DNA. As a result, Caroline's DNA-safeguarding mechanisms kicked in, and caused her to duplicate or copy the complete section of chromosome 22 that she had received correctly from one of us, and replace the absent section with the duplicated material. This could be identified by tests; these discovered a large section of the chromosome with identical DNA on both the maternal and paternal chromosomes, which would be impossible normally. This indicated that a duplication of the available DNA had occurred to fill in the gap, as it were.

The implications of this diagnosis are that Caroline is essentially in possession of two sets of identical DNA from one parent on part of chromosome 22, and she is missing the complementary genes from the other parent. It is unknown as yet which parent's DNA is absent, but blood tests will reveal this in the coming year. We are unsure of the significance of this diagnosis and what repercussions it will have for Caroline, as there are currently no known, documented cases of this exact condition to date worldwide. It is known that uniparental disomy on other chromosomes has resulted in serious syndromes with poor outcomes for the children with the condition, but Caroline's positive developmental start is encouraging. That is what we have to focus on now.

Of course, the internet has yielded the usual horror stories of all the potential scenarios of damage in some way to chromosome 22. These scenarios range from a predisposition to cancers, psychiatric conditions and immune-system problems, to a host of others. We have dutifully read and digested all the information and promptly returned to looking after Caroline as a perfectly normal, healthy member of the family. What else can we do? This is the child who was not supposed to be here at all. This is the child who was expected by some to be potentially significantly impaired in many ways, due to her extremely low birth weight at full term. Yet, apart from being small for her age, she is a fully functioning, bright, physically capable little girl full of all the mischief, chat and challenge of any other three-year-old. A diagnosis wished for can often be a mixed blessing when it arrives. In our case, our hopes and theories of a purely structural, non-genetic, placental issue being the reason for the growth restriction have been dashed. It is now a genetic issue for Caroline.

Genes code for every protein in the human body. They dictate every aspect of normal, healthy human development and so any glitches tend to have consequences, however variable. I suppose at this stage we are hoping that her condition will affect only her growth and physical development, which may be improved by growth hormones, and that all other aspects of her development remain on the upward trajectory they have been on since birth. I think she will be okay. I feel it – she has defied the odds too many times before. Caroline is a fighter; she doesn't give up easily and her environment – which plays as important a role as genetics – is a stimulating, positive place where she will, I hope, continue to thrive. We will know more, we hope, in the coming years about the condition, but it comes as no surprise that Caroline is unique. We always knew that anyway!

The care Caroline has received through the public-health system has been second to none. I know this may not be the case for everyone, but we cannot fault the care she has received. More could not have been done for her, and she couldn't have met more professional and talented medical personnel. Her case provides a strong argument for maintaining funding at an adequate level to ensure that we maintain educational standards and continue to produce many more of these exceptional people in the future.

Caroline went for a heart check-up in March 2010 and had echo, ECG and many other heart checks done. Again, we were blessed with the news that her heart was structurally and rhythmically perfect and that the murmur was, as had been mentioned in the neonatal unit, benign and would cause no issues for the future. We have been so lucky, it is unbelievable; I never imagined Caroline could come out of such serious growth retardation apparently unscathed so far. There is always the worry that we will get bad news, but this reduces each day and month that goes by and Caroline is well. The paediatricians have decided to see Caroline now only once or twice a year because there isn't any specific condition to treat until we know more from the most recent DNA tests to find out what genes may be absent maternally or paternally due to the disomy. They just want to keep an eye on her in case her weight stops increasing. Colin and I have been continuously warned that Caroline will be a small adult and a petite woman, but at this point we just nod our heads and say, 'We know.'

What do we really think? Well, we are not going to spend years worrying whether she will be small, and how small, and if she will be teased, and all the other stuff that might happen. We believe Caroline might be small, but then again she might not. It was predicted she might die and she didn't. It was thought she might have a skeletal dysplasia and she didn't. She was predicted by the experts to be a minimum of 1.5 kilograms if she did survive until thirty-six weeks, or 2 kilograms if she made full term. She was much smaller than that and did very well. She was predicted to reach between three and four feet tall, and she was already 2 feet 8 inches (83 centimetres) tall at two-and-a-half years old. This puts her in the bottom 0.4 per cent of the population but on the centiles with the population. Someone has to be on this end of the spectrum or there would be no bottom centiles! I don't know what height Caroline will reach, but one thing is certain: I guarantee, on her past performances she will surprise everybody, because that seems to be her style. Even if she is small, I don't really care. I can see she is arming herself with the personality traits required to stand up for herself if anyone makes rude comments. Colin and I know if all Caroline has to face is relatively short stature, we have done well and it isn't very significant. It is even more reason to take her shopping for nice high heels if she wants them! I know that whatever happens, it is going to be all right: Caroline is going to be fine, just fine.

Clearly, with a firm diagnosis now received, a purely placental explanation for Caroline's health is no longer applicable, and probably was just a part of the growth issues as suggested to us by the specialist earlier in the pregnancy. Although there is no skeletal dysplasia, there is a genetic answer to Caroline's growth and we hope now to be able to learn more about what that will entail for her future as she continues to develop.

18

CAROLINE THE PERSONALITY, NOT THE IUGR BABY

I want to mention a little bit about Caroline the person, not Caroline the IUGR baby or small Caroline. Caroline is the quintessential wild child. Not everybody sees this, of course, because she is adept at putting on the delicate-little-soul act if it can get her her own way. Like any three-year-old, Caroline loves to play, especially outside. From an early age her favourite garden toys were her slide and her bike. We caught Caroline at eighteen months climbing to the top of the slide on the steps and, upon getting to the top, letting go of the handles of the sides and having a good old look at life from five feet up. Before long she was copying her brothers' antics and sliding down head first or backwards squealing with delight. Now she rarely uses the steps at all, preferring to climb up the wrong way and slide back down again. She realised very quickly that lying back – and taking her wellies off – made her go so much faster.

The baby swing with the safety barrier never impressed her, not when there was one with no safety barrier that the boys were on. Even though she hadn't a hope of staying on without help, she would insist on trying to balance on the big 'babas' swing', as she referred to it. When she was one year old and not yet on her feet, she used to try to crawl after her brothers while they played on their tractors and cars. One day, as we were doing a bit of gardening, assuming Caroline was safely playing on a rug with a few toys strewn around her, we heard her laughing with her brothers while they sang 'The wheels on the bus', a song she loves. We came around the corner to see they had made a sort of train. David was on his big toy tractor with Paul attached to the back of him on his toy Unimog car. Samuel was tied to the back of Paul on a digger-type trailer toy and Caroline's head was barely visible, peering over the top of the toy tractor trailer in which they had put her and propped her up with cushions. We got a fabulous picture that day of the four of them like steps of stairs, with David at the helm driving them all along. A halt had to be called soon afterwards, however, when David decided to do a rally-driving version of the game and Caroline was seen up on one wheel coming around the corner at the rear!

Caroline has not missed a hurling session in months, gathering up her hurley and sliothar to join her brothers to the amusement of everyone at the pitch. She cannot understand why she can't join in and insists on running over with Sam to play with the under sixes and trying to take the opposition out with her hurley. She definitely sees its potential as a weapon more than as a piece of sporting equipment. She has been to see her mum, dad and brothers racing in athletics events (our family loves running), and she makes us help her practise her sprint start repeatedly. If we say, 'On your marks,' she puts her hands to her feet with military precision and speed; at 'Get set' she looks up with a beam on her face; and she usually pre-empts 'Go' – as all the greats do – and she's off flying down the track. She was very quick to see the benefits of being a fast runner. In the shopping centres during the weekly shop she would beg to be taken out of the trolley, promising of course to hold Daddy's hand. No sooner would her feet hit the ground than she would cleverly throw her hat in one direction and run the opposite way, leaving Colin dithering as to whether to pick up the hat or chase her first, by which time she had opened up a good lead. She has the makings of a great race walker too; I liken her, petite as she is, to Olive Loughnane, the Irish silver medallist in race walking in the 2009 Athletics World Championships. She loves coming to watch me race walk and always gives a great cheer as I go past, so we'll see.

From an early age she viewed the buggy as her arch enemy: 'Why be pushed when you can walk?' was the attitude. Her attitude to the car seat is similar; she constantly opens the safety catch.

Caroline occasionally suffers from constipation if she does not drink enough while she is running around. Colin and I worked out through experience with the other children that hide-and-seek is a great cure for this ailment. The boys would loudly count to ten in a booming voice while I would grab Caroline's hand and run at breakneck speed behind a door or somewhere, saying, 'Oh no, they're going to find us.' The boys – all pre-warned of course – would do the usual, banging cupboards and stomping up the stairs, nearly finding her but coming back when she least expected it. She would be holding her breath with the excitement mixed with apprehension. A few games of scary hide-and-seek usually resulted in a quick resolution of the constipation, and were fun at the same time.

Nowadays the trampoline – the 'boing' as she used to call it aptly until recently – is her favourite toy. She is lethal on it, throwing herself around and pandering to her brothers' requests to her to do flips, which she dutifully tries at every opportunity. The funniest thing, watching her on the trampoline, is her very fine blond hair getting charged with static very quickly from the friction and standing on end. Lifting her out isn't too much fun afterwards, however, as the shock can be quite savage. She is fond of rugby, possibly due to our avid interest in Munster rugby, and can catch the ball and, of course, run with it if we throw it very gently to her. She hasn't made a bad job of attempting to tackle or scrummage with her brothers either. If she's not out trying to ride her brothers' bikes instead of her own, or their scooters, which are far too big for her, she loves to play 'army' inside. Her brothers love toy soldiers and building model tank and aeroplane kits and then having the inevitable battle afterwards. She is in the thick of it, knocking the armies over much to the annoyance of her brothers. If the boys go outside with their wooden guns, she follows them, shouting, 'Bang, bang, bang.'

Quiet time for Caroline, which tends to be relatively rare, involves her drawing or being read a story. Given the choice, unless she is tired she will spend ages drawing and colouring with her brothers. She is well able to draw her own version of things and explain what it is, which is very cute. Making models with plasticine is very popular, too, and with three brothers addicted to art-related activities, she too has an interest in them, which in no way surprises Colin and me.

Special occasions with Caroline, as with all children, are huge fun. Christmas usually involves having to redecorate the tree up to four or five times as she has a fascination with stripping it bare when our backs are turned. I thought only cats did that, but apparently little girls do as well. On

Christmas Day she usually has more interest in seeing what Santa has brought the boys than in opening her own presents. Hallowe'en is a double celebration in our house because it is also David's birthday, but for the last two years Caroline has chosen to dress up as a witch and insists on going trick-or-treating. She hops into the buggy between houses, under protest of course, and is wheeled like a queen to the next residence. She is a nightmare at birthday parties as, no matter how vigilant we are, she almost always manages to blow out some of the candles or swipe them before the party boy or girl has a chance to. One would imagine that with all these antics she would annoy other kids, including our own. She does at times, but everyone seems to like her and have a natural tolerance for her, even if they don't know anything about her story. She is extremely popular at school pick-up time, with everyone shouting 'Hello' to her. I'm not sure what it was about her – probably her size – but her popularity was a bit annoying at the time when she was just beginning to walk and only looked the age of a seven- or eight-month-old. There would be children everywhere, and they would pick her up and carry her around, which she hated. Sometimes she would actually be plagued by little girls treating her like a little baby or doll and not leaving her to play by herself. Of course, there were also the parents who could tell she was small for her age and who would ask us what age she was and look disbelieving when they heard, encouraging us to tell them more of the story. Depending on whether we felt they were genuinely interested or just being nosey, we would explain that she was very small at birth or else look at them blankly and explain nothing.

Caroline does experience some side effects of her small size in other people's attitudes. With regards to comments directed to children, sometimes I cannot understand the insensitivity of many adults, even sometimes medical professionals we meet for Caroline's check-ups. She is three now and has very good comprehension of language. She is not a baby and, although she is small, she looks more like a little girl now than a baby. I can understand to some degree adults who don't know Caroline making comments, but it can still be somewhat annoying. So many, whether they know Caroline or not, comment, 'Oh, she's gorgeous, she's tiny. She's like a little doll.' When she was younger and didn't understand I could tolerate this, but now it's getting harder. Caroline answered me recently when I told her that she was a big girl now and needed to have her hair tied up and out of her eyes, 'No Mama. I'm not big. I'm small.' I sat down with her and told her she was getting bigger all the time and she looked at me as if everyone except me knew that she was small.

I don't want her to grow up feeling different and I think the age of three is very early to be learning this. Children say a lot less; it's adults who comment on her size. It's hard to know what to do because I don't want to fall out with people, but to me this is disrespectful, and when they do it when Caroline's with me, I want to say, 'Please don't make comments about her appearance because she knows what you are saying.' But if I make a fuss I feel I will probably make more of an issue out of it with Caroline, which will make her even more conscious of it. On bad days, when they announce, 'Oh, she's tiny, look at her,' I do sometimes want to retort, 'Yes, and look at yours. They've a fair bit of fat on them, haven't they?' But of course this would be cruel to the child and I would never do it. It would not be considered acceptable, yet commenting on Caroline's appearance seems to be okay. All I can hope is that our family develops her confidence so that she will find her own way of responding in her own time. I look forward to the day she answers back in defence when someone makes a personal comment. No doubt she will come across as cheeky or indignant, but I won't be calling her on it, not when the adult should know better in the first place.

Speaking of confidence and personality traits, most people who meet Caroline say she is a Doran (my maiden name) in nature. I usually say, 'Do you think so?' in a trying-to-hide-my-delight kind of way. They then go on to say, admiringly usually, how stubborn she is or how it's her way or no way, or how she's very feisty and has a temper. I am not insulted about that because it's true and she is very like me. Her stubbornness was evident from early on when she wouldn't let me feed her because she wanted to do it, even when she wasn't able yet. Or when I refused to let her out of the high chair to sit at the table because we had to put so many cushions under her she was too unbalanced and I was frightened she would fall. What did she do when I turned my back when she was fifteen months old? She somehow opened or squeezed out of the high-chair straps, stood up and took a step right over the side, landing on her head on the tiled floor. Miraculously she didn't do major damage, but our saying 'No' just seems to encourage her to find a way herself.

She is both stubborn and very determined. I remember watching her taking a tiny Lego man's hat on and off continuously until she was able to do it without dropping the hat. The same thing happened with putting shapes in a ball-shaped toy with spaces for them. She wasn't inclined to give up when a shape wouldn't go in or to come to ask us to put it in for her. She would give it a good manoeuvre until she managed, or else fire it across the room in a temper as if the problem was with it and not her. I could never just pick up any old book lying around to read her a story. She would say, 'No, not this one, I ate [hate] this one, I go get my one,' meaning 'the one I want'. She would never get waylaid, either, on a mission. Back she would come with her book and dump it on my lap, saying, 'Read it', while she clambered up onto my lap.

When Caroline interacts with other children she is the boss, regardless of their age. She is confident and feisty and has been known to get her own way through any means possible. She also has a wicked sense of humour. She will hide visiting children's soothers in the toy boxes in the playroom and claim innocently she knows nothing about them, until she is seen returning with them later when the protestations of the other children get too much for her. I am not proud to admit she has had all three of her brothers reduced to tears at some stage, either through frustration because she is wrecking their game or because they haven't included her and she has come up stealthily behind them and hit them with her toy lightsaber (she loves *Star Wars*). They always forgive her, however, because they really do love her. The first thing they do every morning, if she hasn't woken them up first, is go and give her a big kiss. She, in characteristic form, usually tries to push them away, saying, 'Yuck' – long may this continue! If they hassle her they get a slap. That's how it is; they know the score. They also know the score with her size, although they no longer even register her size at all. They all remember their trips into the neonatal unit, which they hated because it was so boring for them and at that time, as they say, 'Caroline was no fun then like she is now.' They are extremely patient with her, and I suppose they let her get away with a lot more than they let each other get away with. All three boys have said they are going to look out for her in the yard at school and if they see anyone being mean to her or teasing her, they will tell the teachers immediately. I have my suspicions that they'll call the teachers only after offering some verbal interventions of their own! Yes, they do adore Caroline; they think she is brilliant fun and very mischievous, which she is.

I wouldn't like to portray Caroline as a precocious or bold child, although there is no doubt she has benefited from a distinct mellowing of our parental discipline, both as we have become more relaxed and experienced about parenting over the years, but also because of her circumstances. She isn't spoiled in the material sense, nor is she allowed to get away with bold behaviour such as hitting, but, because she is so adept at doing something funny in the midst of a misdemeanour, she usually diffuses the situation by making us laugh. Caroline is the only one of our children to do the tantrum; she throws herself on the ground and rolls around screaming, but never at the shops – she's too busy running away! If Caroline is bold and she senses we are cross with her, the response can vary depending on her mood and how cross she thinks we are. I know we are not supposed to shout at children but we do a lot of the time when they misbehave. As Colin says, it's the only way to get them to listen sometimes. Caroline is very good at gauging the mood. On the one hand, if we raise our voices but are not really angry, just putting it on, she will take us off and shout back some gibberish in an attempt at an authoritative tone, as if to point out that that's what we're doing. If, on the other hand, she knows we are really cross and that she is wrong, she will voluntarily say, 'Sorry,' and walk to the naughty step we have at the bottom of the stairs and do her time. If she is upset, she might then howl, or drop her bottom lip if she is just sad about it.

Caroline has a great knack of gauging a situation or mood or person's feelings. She has regularly come to Colin or me when we have been tired or in bad form and asked quietly, 'Are you happy?' She would never ask, 'Are you sad?' as if she doesn't want us to be, yet she knows if we are. Often she will climb up and give us a really big cuddle (not a kiss, however) and just lie there quietly with us for a while.

Bedtimes with Caroline are still hit and miss. She did well for a long time, but when she is sick she insists on someone sleeping with her and it can take weeks to get her back on the usual track again. Like everything, she is well able to manipulate this situation. When she was smaller she used to cry when she was put into her cot, and if we just did the supernanny thing, saying, 'Goodnight' and walking out, she would tell us she was feeling sick. We would then need to go back to her because feeding her was too difficult to risk her losing the lot. When we returned she would be smiling victoriously, and we would then tell her she was not sick and leave again. The only problem was that if she wanted to, she could easily wind herself up until she *did* vomit up all her bottle and evening's food. For this reason she has been indulged more at bedtime than the other children were. We've tried to balance some level of discipline, but simultaneously keep her calories in, and unfortunately she has sussed that one out. She is less able to make herself sick now, as she is older – I suppose her digestive system is less delicate – so we sometimes hear her coughing to try to be sick and it doesn't work, even if she is quite upset.

She does eventually find a way to get us up to go to her, however. One trick which always makes me laugh – Colin less so – is when she calls, 'Cooolin,' from the cot. It is lost on none of the family that she is mimicking me when I am calling Colin for something. Caroline reckons if he comes to me when I shout for him, there is a good chance he will come to her. Colin just raises his eyes to heaven as if to say, 'Not another one.' Lately she has taken to asking Colin early in the evening if he will come up to bed with her. He usually makes up some excuse – such as he will have to feed the dog first – and says he might go up afterwards. If she does fall asleep and then wakes during the night, she will call him and ask him nicely if she can come in beside him. Sometimes she will say she is cold and needs a warm daddy. Of course, this is hard to resist so nine times out of ten he goes into her room with her. I sometimes say to her I need a warm daddy too, but she says, 'No you don't,' with a huge grin on her face. Because Colin is Caroline's at-home parent, she looks to him for many of her needs and they do have a special bond. It can sometimes be a bit hard for me when she goes to him before me, but it also has its distinct advantages, especially at night, when I am able to say, 'But she's calling for you, Colin!'

Caroline is a tomboy with a strong feminine streak too, if that makes sense. What I mean is that she loves the rough-and-tumble life at home with the boys, would far rather be outside than inside, plays mainly boys' games and has no interest in dolls – all of which is understandable as she has three brothers as her main playmates. She is brave and daring too – even more so than the boys, which is a surprise. One distinct difference that I feel I could legitimately put down to her feminine side is that she loves her bath and being clean and having her teeth and hands cleaned, once she has finished playing. It's not a chore for her to come in and be cleaned, like it is with the boys. She finds it enjoyable and feels nice after a bath. Of course, she has a great time playing in there with her brothers too. She'll even willingly let us wash her hair so it smells nice, which is a huge no-no with the boys. She is similar with clothes. The boys could take or leave clothes, with the exception of Paul, who has an eye for what looks good. Caroline will religiously pick what she wants to wear for the day. It could as easily be her jeans or a dress; it's all down to how she feels on that particular morning. If she doesn't want to wear something we have picked out, she will tell us she can't wear that as it's dirty. She has an answer for everything and always has to get the last word – okay, yes, I hear that, me too! For a party it has to be a party dress; nothing else will do.

When we decided to train Caroline out of nappies, Colin got the new knickers out to show her what she would be wearing in a few weeks and she wore a frilly pink pair on her head all day, as if to say, 'You know what you can do with those.' She then had the potty hoisted up on her head where the knickers had been. It was an eventful few weeks' potty training!

She often giggles at the sight of me when I get out of the shower – I can't blame her! I tell her she used to drink milk from mommy's boobs when she asks what they are, to which she replies that she'll have pink ones when she's bigger. If that's not the height of femininity, surely nothing is!

It is very hard to say whether, intellectually, there will be repercussions from her experience in the womb. I suppose we won't know that until she goes to school. All the signs at the moment are indicating that her development is very age-appropriate, which is encouraging. Caroline knows all the colours and can count some of the way to ten. She tends to go well up to five and then say seven, eight and nine; she doesn't seem to like six. We haven't taught her any of this, however; she is just picking it up from the boys. She has good speech but her pronunciation isn't perfect on some words; we can understand almost everything she says. She is hilarious when we don't understand what she is saying. She will say it, we will get it wrong, and for a few guesses she will politely say, 'No' and say it again. If, after that, we still don't understand, she will patronisingly try to spell it out for us in slower speech, for example: 'Will you o … pen the do … or … for … meee.' Alternatively, if she is in particularly good form, she will laugh at our guesses as if to say, 'You are quite stupid at times, aren't you?' So we think she is bright enough for her age. We did read that IUGR babies can have sensory issues, such as hating loud noises, or that they can be extremely fractious and fussy. There is no indication of this in Caroline so far. She would be in serious trouble in our house if she had an issue with lots of noise, however, and overall she is a contented and easy-going little girl most of the time, and is demanding but lovely with it.

Caroline continues to amaze us with her progressive attitude to trying and doing things. She is in a big girl's bed now – lacking the constraining bars of a cot – and has not yet realised that a journey downstairs after bedtime is a possibility. There is no doubt that in the coming weeks this dawning realisation will result in the patter of her little feet creeping down for another story. She has demanded that her room be painted pink and says she needs 'Hello Kitty' covers for her bed. As she snuggles down to sleep, her bed adorned with all her 'pets' (as she calls her cuddly toys, just like her brother Sam), she already looks very grown up compared to merely months ago. She incessantly talks about going to school and regularly finds her backpack to bring with her, when the boys are being dropped off at school, in the hope that soon one of the teachers might invite her in and let her stay. She has discovered the joys of the box of make-up and nail varnish; the gaudy results are to be seen all over both Caroline and the bathroom floor. She is at that stage – which is all too familiar to parents of toddlers – that I call the 'split lip' stage, involving an obsession with jumping on sofas, beds or anything with a spring in it. The tooth fairy will have little trade in our house in the coming years unless Caroline gets over the superwoman stage soon! Of course, Colin and I wouldn't have it any other way; we are enjoying every minute, whether nerve-racking or entertaining, with her.

Caroline knows a lot about herself and her start in life, but I don't know how much of it she understands. In the hall of our house there are pictures of our four children, all taken on the day they were born, and each displayed with a coin from the year the child was born. I think Caroline knows she had tubes and treatment that the others didn't, because when she passes her picture she tells me that's when she was sick in hospital. We tell her how we used to visit her in hospital and she tells us the doctor put a needle in her hand, but that's most likely remembered from her last bout in hospital. When she was with Colin and her granny in Scotland, and I was talking to her on the phone, she asked me if I was still writing a book about her. She had been upset that I wasn't going to Scotland with them, so I had told her why I needed to stay behind: because I was writing a book about her. As she gets older we can tell her more and more of the story, including the toughest part – all about our trip abroad. We haven't broached how that should be tackled yet, but I will get advice on the best age and approach to tackle it. I do intend to tell her, however, because I wouldn't want to keep it from her and I feel the need to be honest with her about our intense fear and mindset at that time. We will need to talk to the boys about that too, probably sooner rather than later.

It has been an experience with intense ups and downs but it is a story with a remarkably happy ending. We have Caroline home with us and her brothers, to enjoy and to love. She demonstrated the will to fight to be with us against incredibly poor odds and she succeeded. She is our beautiful, special, perfect, and sweet little girl. We love you so much, Caroline, and always will.

19

REFLECTION

Sometimes I sit and think, 'I can't believe 2008 is over and we survived it, and Caroline survived it too.' Sometimes it seems as if the whole thing didn't happen to us at all, but to people we used to know in a parallel universe. The whole year was so stressful we almost disengaged from real life and passed time only worrying and focusing on Caroline. Sadly, I have few memories of the boys and what they were up to that year. The photos of that time show the strain the whole family was under, even the children, who didn't fully understand what was happening. It's difficult to contemplate how, literally, one minute life could have been good – I mean really good – and the next minute have been falling down around us, or so it seemed. It did at times seem like a 'year from hell', but it couldn't have ended on a better note, because Caroline was born and survived, so it would be unfair to give it that label.

I remember, night after night, I used to plague Colin, asking him if he thought Caroline would make it. I don't know whether it was due to his positive nature or simply for my benefit, but he always said he felt she would be okay. Does hopefulness exude a kind of positivity that can swing things towards a good outcome, or is it all just science? Is there a real power in prayer? Why did Caroline survive when the odds were stacked so much against her? Was it Caroline who never gave up or was she conscious at all of anything that was happening? These are some of the many questions that go round my head when I have a quiet moment to think back and be thankful to whomever – God, or the doctors, or was it fate or simply luck on our side?

I constantly reflect on the times when I was at my lowest and Caroline would start dancing as if to tell me she was there and never to give up on her, never to give up hope. I never did either; even when we went away for those awful days I don't think I would ever have followed through. I needed to go, out of some sort of test of myself, some sort of assessment of my own moral purpose in life. I know there will be people who will judge me and possibly Colin (but probably me because I am a mother) on what we set out to do. One thing I have learned through this experience is that people don't fully know themselves until they are faced with something dark, something very difficult, that challenges everything they think they know. Of course, I wish now

I had never had to accept that I thought about letting Caroline go. It's almost harder when I look at how perfect she is and imagine what an awful, awful thing it would have been if she had died at our behest. But if she were in terrible pain now with a skeletal dysplasia that meant she was in a life of torment from birth, would that have been any more awful or still the same wrong decision? I don't know. I am just glad we didn't give up hope and that we had the guts to face whatever child we got, regardless of disability, but that was a hard decision to make and we needed to explore whether we could come to that final point by almost testing ourselves. We are not perfect people and we were scared. That just about sums it up.

Colin and I did a lot of speculating and thinking during the pregnancy, along the lines of, 'I wonder what will have happened this time next month or next year or in two years.' Normally when we do that we forget we ever did it, but with Caroline we remembered. The day she was born we said, 'Remember all the times we wondered if this day would ever come?' We kept saying this, and still do. It's important because we feel so grateful that she is with us and we want to acknowledge continually that we have her alive and well at home with us. Did the year strengthen Colin and me as a partnership? I know one thing: we were there for each other throughout the year, really there for each other. But afterwards, while we have been coming down from the whole experience, we realise it has changed us, and I think we need to remember that we were both in this thing together, but both of us have changed, so the relationship is different and it takes time to adapt to that. I also think that after an experience like we had it is possible to be frightened to be happy afterwards. We had been stressed and worried for so long that those feelings don't just up and leave when things get better; we have to work at it. I often wonder if humankind is a bit on the ambitious side when we say all we want is to be happy and for our children to be happy in whatever they end up doing. Isn't being happy a state of mind or emotion like being sad? So it makes no sense to expect to be happy all the time, as that would be as bland as being stuck in any one state of emotion all the time. The emotional roller coaster is a necessary part of a healthy and happy human experience, in my view, although it often isn't easy to deal with. There are times and things that make a person happy, just as there are times and things that make a person sad or angry or surprised or proud. We almost think there is something wrong with us if we are not happy all the time, yet if we were sad all the time we would see a doctor to do something about it. So Colin and I are not always happy and that's okay and normal, I feel, but we are content a lot of the time and that is a much more stable place to be for us. Contented is somewhere in the middle of happy and sad, and every day there are moments of happiness and sadness as we talk about and reflect on our journey. I think we are in a good place, and I strongly feel things will even get better as time passes. It's that hopefulness again that Caroline brought out in us, and which before I had her was not there a lot of the time, even when things appeared to be just fine. We thank Caroline for that and so much more.

We still don't know all the answers about what happened to Caroline and not having certain answers poses its own issues. I worry about what might be lurking in the future. I know I shouldn't worry, but I think worrying is a mother's prerogative. Every day we see Caroline progress and do something funny or new, the worries fade a little bit. We sometimes wonder if we have had our share of bad luck now. We joke that it should do us a good few years at least, but we know others have it much tougher. We saw this in the hospitals we frequented during the pregnancy and have been to since Caroline was born. There are people who have had a much tougher time than we have, and they are coping. We rarely wonder about things such as what Caroline will be when she grows up, as we did with the boys as their personalities developed. I am not sure why that is. Perhaps we need to see how she continues to develop first. I do feel very strongly that Caroline will lead a blessed life, a very content and fulfilled life. I just feel that. She deserves it because she was so brave and such a determined baby to pull through. I do believe that every child is special in his or her own way, but Caroline has something extra special about her. I think everyone sees it. Maybe I'm wrong, but I think Caroline is different to other children. She is; you'll just have to take my word for it. So to families out there going through something awful too: don't give up hope and always listen to your gut instincts. Caroline told me all along she would be okay. If I had listened to her and only her, I would have saved myself so much heartache.

The importance of friends and family cannot be understated. We would have found it even harder had people not been there for us. Whether it was their talking to us or waiting for us to talk, or just from a look, we knew people cared and we are very grateful. But the worst is over, we hope, and we do need to put it behind us and start laughing a hell of a lot more. There is no doubt that Caroline will be instrumental in ensuring that. We have lots to look forward to and the way time is flying we need to tune right in and savour all the days we spend with our children and each other. I am very conscious we need to give ourselves a pat on the back too and tell each other how well we did, because no one can really imagine how soul-destroying it was at times when we were told that Caroline might not make it. We must again thank our consultant for his patience and ability to see the bigger picture in giving Caroline the best chance of a healthy life. Keeping Caroline or us buoyed up and alive was, and still is to some extent, a team effort, with a huge number of people playing a role along the way. We feel so relieved and so lucky. Caroline our daughter is with us; she is well and happy and having the time of her life after a terrible start. Long may it continue for our special and sweet Caroline.